THE WOK—AS OLD AS TIME...
AS NEW AS TOMORROW....

Scramble an egg in seconds or cook for a crowd in a jiffy. The wonderful wok is the most versatile, easy-to-use utensil that ever found its way into American kitchens.

Master chef Ceil Dyer shows you how to use the four basic cooking methods, how to slice and chop foods for ultra-efficiency, how to clean and care for your wok, how to rate the twelve most popular brands and select the electric or stove-top wok that's just right for you.

From Sukiyaki to Sweet & Sour Shrimp, from Potatoes O'Brien to Noodles & Sausage Napoli, you'll find that meats stay juicy, seafoods keep their delicate flavor and vegetables cook to perfection. You'll discover how easy it is to whip up a meal or entertain a crowd with *Wok Cookery*.

D0483614

WOK COOKERY

Ceil Dyer

A DELL BOOK

Published by
Dell Publishing Co., Inc.
1 Dag Hammarskjold Plaza
New York, New York 10017

© 1977 H. P. Books

Dell ® TM 681510, Dell Publishing Co., Inc.

ISBN: 0-440-19663-9

Reprinted by arrangement with H.P. Books.

Printed in the United States of America

First Dell printing—September 1981

Sixth printing—September 1983

Eighth printing—December 1984

CONTENTS

WHY A WOK?

We are all pretty much in the same boat these days: rich, not so rich or like me. As with most people, making a living takes most of my time. I'm interested in good nutrition and into "gourmet" food but I'm often low on cash and time. That's why I've turned to wok cookery. It's the total answer; an implement almost as old as time but as new as tomorrow.

With this one pot I can scramble an egg or cook for a crowd. I can prepare "good for you" meals, interesting, quick and inexpensive meals—all at the same time. It goes back to basics and on to the most elegant cuisine. It's right for today's way of life. It's a fuel saver, a money and time saver. It's a pot with seemingly endless uses. You'll love it.

The Chinese invented the wok but it should not be used only to prepare Chinese food. Far from it! The wok is a versatile utensil that lends itself to an infinite variety of recipes. Do you know *why* the Chinese invented the wok? To save fuel. Its unique shape heats faster and uses less fuel to maintain a high temperature.

For thousands of years the wok's unique shape has remained exactly the same. No one has found a way to improve it. If you could own but one cooking pot it would have to be a wok. Stir-frying, the first method that comes to mind for wok cookery, is only the beginning. Deep-fat frying, braising and steaming, are all easier, faster and better tasting from the magical wok. And, clean-up time is reduced to minutes. Once seasoned, a wok needs only a fast rinse and thorough drying.

Perhaps the most wonderful thing about wok cookery is the decided improvement in taste of even ordinary foods. The high heat cooks rapidly and heightens the flavor of your ingredients. Meats are brown but still juicy. Seafood retains its delicate flavor; vegetables stay fresh-tasting. Moreover, foods keep their color; each dish is a feast for the eye as well as the palate. Ingredients can be prepared ahead, refrigerated until ready to use and an entire meal prepared in a few minutes. It makes exciting, really good food with less work and effort than any other method I know.

For example, try Veal & Peppers Romano, page 179, with crusty Italian bread and plenty of grated Parmesan cheese. End with fresh fruit, espresso coffee and pass a plate of Italian chocolate. Easy? Of course!

Or serve New Orleans Jambalaya, page 138. Combined with rice, this needs only a light dessert to make a memorable meal.

Entertaining comes easy with a wok. You can cook at the table with the electric versions or with your conventional wok on a portable burner designed to hold the wok securely. Used at the table or not, a wok looks good on the most attractive buffet.

The wok can come to your rescue if you are calorie conscious. It uses very little oil, even for stir-frying, and steamed dishes really help "zero" the calorie count. Incredibly, even deep-fried foods can be enjoyed with a clear conscience. The intense heat seals the batter quickly so very little oil is absorbed into the food.

The wok inspires a gourmet range of desserts, from delicate Mocha Sponge Cake, page 265, to Down-East Indian Pudding, page 234. All easy and effortless, and each one a pleasure to make and eat.

I know you will enjoy these recipes. I carefully tested each one, then my good friend Elsie Pearce retested them. I tried to use only readily available ingredients. I know too well the frustration of an interesting recipe that uses ingredients you can't find.

WOK COOKERY METHODS

This is not a book of exotic Oriental dishes. The methods of cooking are authentic Chinese or adaptations of those used by Oriental cooks; however, all of the ingredients should be available in your markets and the recipes are derived from many cuisines.

Stir-Frying

Stir-frying comes first to mind, the art of *Chao: High heat—shallow oil—continual stirring—quick frying of cut-up ingredients with wet or dry seasoning.* This applies whether your ingredients are for an authentic Chinese dish or a country-style stew.

Meats for stir-frying are always either ground or cut in thin strips. Vegetables such as carrots, onions and green peppers are either diced or cut wafer-thin. Leafy vegetables such as spinach or lettuce are simply shredded or torn into bite-size pieces.

The key to stir-frying success is to have everything ready *before* you begin. Cooking time is so short there is simply no chance to stop and look for ingredients.

I like to use peanut oil, the Chinese chefs' favorite for a very good reason: It can be heated to a high temperature without smoking and its bland taste doesn't overpower the flavor of the dish. *Never substitute solid shortening, butter or margarine for the oil.*

Steaming

Steaming is the most subtle form of wok cookery. Like most Americans I never thought of steaming as an Oriental cooking method and in my pre-wok days, steaming—except for puddings—sounded dull. The Chinese practiced *feong*—steam cookery—for thousands of years and brought it to gourmet perfection.

The food to be steamed is arranged in a shallow heat-proof dish on a rack in the wok over, *not in*, simmering water—or the food is placed directly on the rack. The wok is then covered and steam does the rest. Easy? Of course! Just two points to remember: Be sure to have the water simmering *before* placing the dish on the steaming rack. In some recipes, a piece of aluminum foil is placed loosely over the food to prevent condensation from falling into the dish.

Wok steaming has an almost magical way of heightening food flavor. The delicate flavor of fish isn't lost in the cooking process. When seasoned with a bit of imagination, it's delicious. Vegetables keep their color and fresh taste. They are almost too pretty to eat. And steamed poultry can be an epicurean dish. Try the recipe for steamed Cornish Game Hens California-Style on page 96. It's only one delectable sample of wok-steamed cookery.

The reason you will find wok steaming so easy and so good is the unique ability of a wok to retain high heat.

Foods cook amazingly fast without excessive loss by shrinkage. Instead of drying out, meats and poultry remain colorful, flavorful and juicy. Super-easy and super-fast, you can steam an entire meal in your wok with delicious results and almost no clean-up time. And, steaming really helps the calorie-counter, too.

Place the food to be steamed on a rack in your wok. The water under the rack should be simmering. Then cover the wok.

Before preparing a steamed recipe, carefully measure the pan or baking dish you plan to use to make sure it fits on top of the rack in your covered wok. Shallow, wide utensils fit better than deep ones. The size and shape of the utensil you use depends on the size and shape of your wok.

Braising

Braising is also of Oriental lineage. This is the classic *red cooking* of China which takes its name from the deep reddish-brown color of the cooked meat. It is a highly satisfactory way to cook meat. Even the least-expensive cuts become tender and flavorful and a braised fillet of beef is simply a feast for the gods. When meat is braised it doesn't shrink as in roasting—an important point to remember when you ask the price of that fillet.

Easy and effortless, braising is simply a matter of browning the meat in a little oil. The meat should be at room-temperature and blotted thoroughly dry before browning. After browning, it is removed from the wok. Seasoning and vegetables are added to the wok and stir-fried briefly. The meat is placed over the stir-fried vegetables, cooking liquid poured in, the wok covered and the whole left to simmer until the meat is tender. An occasional turning is all that is necessary. Other vegetables may be added during the last half hour of cooking for a complete one-dish meal. Braised meat is delicious hot or cold and highly desirable for stir-fry dishes with the flavorful cooking liquid. Not a scrap goes to waste.

Deep-Frying

Deep-frying is especially fun to do and the results are so spectacular the food simply vanishes from the platter. I avoided deep-frying for years. It seemed like a messy job; it used a lot of expensive oil and the foods were often greasy and calorie-laden. All these objections vanished when the wok came into my life. The wok's shape prevents spatters; it needs only about three cups of oil for a 14-inch or

16-inch wok, and this is reusable. The intense heat seals the food so fast that no flavor escapes into the oil—even fish fried in the Oriental manner leaves no fishy taste in the oil. Most importantly—foods are delicately crisp, and there is absolutely no trace of greasiness. Naturally there are less added calories with this frying method.

Ice-cold foods cooked in hot oil will be crisp and flavorful.

Before measuring oil for deep-frying, check the wok manufacturer's directions for the recommended amount of oil. This depends on the size and shape of your wok.

Secrets of Oriental deep-fry are simple: have the foods and batter ice-cold and the oil hot—375°F (191°C) on a deep-fat thermometer. Peanut oil is used because it will not smoke like other oils at this temperature. Foods such as one- or two-bite-size whole shrimp, scallops, cubes of fish fillets, slices of zucchini, carrots, green onions, cauliflower and broccoli flowerets are dipped in batter with kitchen tongs, lowered immediately into the hot oil, then cooked briefly until golden. Croquettes and fritters are left refrigerated until the moment of frying. The only exception is Beignets, page 264, which are fried in very hot fat as soon as the dough has risen. All foods are drained on paper towels. After that it's only a matter of watching them disappear from the platter—and that takes only a few moments.

HOW TO SLICE & CHOP FOR STIR-FRYING

The short cooking time typical of most all stir-fry dishes is made possible by the way the raw ingredients are sliced, diced, minced or chopped. The original purpose was to compensate for a scarcity of fuel and heat in ancient China. By proper cutting, the food can be brought close to tenderness before it goes in your wok. The characteristics of each ingredient determine the method of cutting.

The major ingredients in a stir-fry dish are generally cut to the same size and shape so they will cook quickly and all be ready to eat at the same time. They are also cut with a critical eye for appearance. The dish should not only taste good but also look appetizing—a joy to behold.

Angled Slicing—One method for tenderizing is angled slicing. Foods prepared in this manner also make a very appetizing and beautiful dish. Any vegetable can be used. Place on the chopping board, hold cleaver at a 45-degree angle and cut across the vegetable.

To Slice Meat Thinly—Place the meat in the freezer compartment of your refrigerator until very firm. Using a razor-sharp knife, slice across the grain as thin as possible. To tenderize further, hold the slice at each end and gently stretch it a bit, taking care not to pull too hard, which could tear it apart.

Diagonal Slicing—Tough steaks and other tough, fibrous meats and vegetables are cut diagonally to tenderize them and to expose the largest possible area to heat. The only difference between this and straight-across slicing is that the cleaver is held away from you at a 45-degree angle to the food. This produces thinnest-possible slices, contributing to fast cooking.

How to Make Beautiful Vegetables

Thin Slicing—Cut through the vegetables to show the direction of the grain. This is the best way to slice fresh mushrooms.

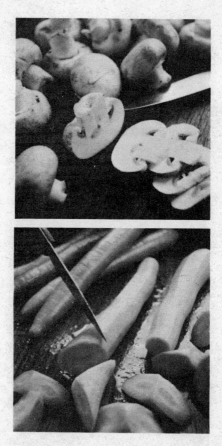

Slice in Diamond Shapes—Roll long vegetables like green onions, celery or carrots as you make diagonal cuts.

Make Pie-Slice Sections—Cut round or cylindrical vegetables in half the long way. Cut through the center of each half. Then cut in slices the same width and separate in pie-shaped wedges.

To Dice—Cut in thin slices, pile the slices one on another and cut them across in fine strips, cut strips across and dice. To dice an onion, cut it from top to bottom. Place cut side down on chopping board, and cut across first vertically—then horizontally.

Dice in Cubes—First cut across, then line up and cut checkerboard fashion in fine cubes.

For Matchstick-Thin Strips—First cut in thin slices, then pile the slices up and cut in thin strips.

Four to Garnish

Green Onion Brushes—Trim root, cut off tip, leaving 3 inches of stalk. Make four crisscross cuts 1-inch deep into both ends of stalk.

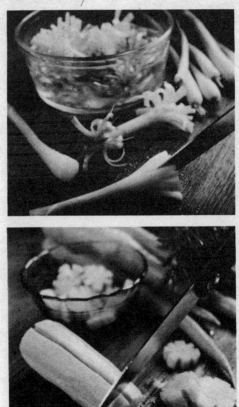

Carrot Flowers—Peel skin off a thick carrot, cut out V-shaped wedges lengthwise, spacing equally all around the carrot. Cut in 1/8-inch-thick pin-wheels.

Fan Cut—Nice and easy to do with zucchini or cucumbers. Trim off ends of vegetable, then cut horizontally in 1/2-inch slices. Cut slices horizontally about 1/4-inch apart, leaving about 1/2-inch intact at one end.

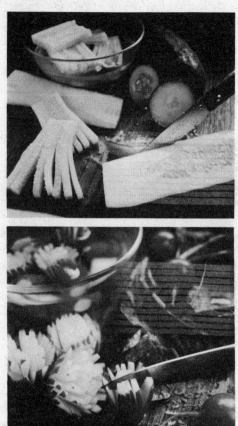

Chrysanthemum Cut—Perfect for radishes or tiny purply-white turnips. Peel top half of vegetable, then make fine checkerboard cuts through tops, leaving bottom of vegetable intact. Place in an ice-water bath. Add a little lemon juice and let stand until ready to drain and use.

CLEANING & CARING FOR YOUR WOK

Just as there are wine snobs who bore everyone in sight with their jumble of vintages, obscure vineyards and so on, there are "pot snobs," those well-meaning, but misguided souls who become very upset if their omelet pan is used for sautéing an onion and even more troubled if it is washed in soapy water. Well, there is no need for all of this—especially not for a wok as it is one of the simplest of all utensils to use and to clean.

But first things first: When you get your new wok home it should be seasoned before you use it. Seasoning is a simple job, far less complicated than the "pot snobs" would have you believe. Here is the easy method for cleaning and seasoning a rolled-steel non-electric wok. First you must remove the machine-oil coating applied by the manufacturer to prevent rust. Immerse the wok in very hot soapy water and soak it for about an hour. Pour in boiling water once or twice to keep the water hot. Drain the wok and clean both inside and out with a scouring pad to remove the last traces of machine oil. Rinse well with very hot water. Dry the wok on a wok ring over a burner set at medium heat. With the burner still on, pour in about 2 teaspoons of peanut oil or vegetable oil other than corn oil. Rub the oil into the wok surface with clean paper towels. Repeat this oiling and rubbing two or three times. Wipe with a clean paper towel.

To clean after cooking simply wash with hot water and detergent. Rinse well and place over medium heat to evaporate all moisture. Rub a teaspoon of oil onto the surface with paper towels.

If your wok is electric, seasoning and cleaning are equally easy. However, a few guidelines apply especially to electric woks. First and most important *always remove heat control before starting to clean your wok*. Then soak your electric wok just as you would the conventional type. Do not use scouring pads on the non-stick interior. If stubborn food sticks, try a plastic-type scrubbing pad. Dry thoroughly, especially the heat-control socket. Rub the cooking surface with 2 teaspoons of oil and your electric wok is ready to use. To clean an electric wok, *first detach heat control*. Wash in hot soapy water using plastic-type pad. The wok may look clean but tiny food particles may adhere to the non-stick finish and must be removed. Dry thoroughly and rub interior with a teaspoon of oil. Be sure heat-control socket is completely dry before reinserting heat control.

Conventional steel woks with a non-stick interior finish are seasoned and cleaned just like an electric one. So you see that's all there is to it for keeping the most versatile of all kitchen utensils ready to go at a moment's notice.

Cleaning your wok accessories is even easier. Your wok may be purchased as a set, complete with a tall lid and a rack for steaming as well as a perforated metal ring to hold the wok securely over your stove burner, or these may be purchased separately. They require no special cleaning, the rack and ring can go in the dish washer if desired and the aluminum steaming lid is simply washed in hot soapy water, rinsed and dried. Don't wash the lid in the dish washer because the drying heat can ruin wooden or plastic knobs.

I store my wok in the open on the kitchen counter. It's

decorative and handy but most important it stays fresh and ready to use. Any oil will become rancid if stored in a dark warm place for a prolonged period and your wok has been seasoned with oil. Do you know this is true of any seasoned steel or iron utensil? This is why many kitchens have an overhead rack where all the pots and pans are hung.

The Right Tool for the Task

You probably already own the "tools" you will need for successful wok cookery for they are simple everyday kitchen equipment.

First on the list is a good chopping board and a sharp—I mean *really* sharp—cleaver, essential for preparing vegetables and slicing meats for stir-fry.

For tossing foods being stir-fried I like to use two long-handled wooden spoons or a Chinese spatula and stirring spoon.

A wire whisk is indispensable to me. Nothing will beat an egg or smooth out a batter like an inexpensive wire whisk.

For deep-fry you will want a skimmer as well as a slotted spoon to remove foods from the hot oil. A pair of kitchen tongs is helpful to lift foods from the batter into the oil. Also, almost essential, a deep-fat thermometer makes deep-frying much more accurate.

For cakes you will want a six-cup ring mold, plus a 5½" x 9½" x 2" loaf pan and a cake rack.

An electric blender and an electric mixer are nice to have. Of the two, I think a blender is most important. You can use a rotary beater and a wooden spoon to mix and stir.

Finally, don't forget a couple of big pot holders. Every well-equipped kitchen deserves them!

BUYER'S GUIDE

There are many woks on the market and they all have the same classic shape. This is as it should be; why tamper with perfection?

Woks are available with non-stick or non-rust finishes; there are electric woks, skillet-type woks with a flat bottom, complete wok sets including a spatula, stirring spoon, skimmer, steamer, even chopsticks and a bamboo scrubbing brush. There are special portable burners for woks. It seems nothing has been forgotten to help you enjoy cooking with a wok.

Basic wok equipment is the wok itself, a burner ring to hold it securely on the stove, a steaming rack and a cover. Beyond this it's up to you to decide what accessories you need. They are usually available separately so you can start with basic equipment and add accessories as you like.

In this section are woks that are currently available in department stores and gourmet shops. Choose one to fit your needs and, with your purchase safely home, you can embark on the happiest of kitchen adventures—*Wok Cookery.*

Conventional Wok by Atlas Metal Spinning™, South San Francisco, CA. *14-inch diameter, two-quart capacity, tempered-steel wok, non-stick finish. Steel handles riveted to base. Aluminum dome lid, plastic knob. Angled ring base.*

Six-piece Wok Set by Schiller & Asmus. *14-inch diameter, two-quart capacity wok of tempered steel, aluminum lid, plastic knob. Steel handles riveted to base. Sawtooth-edged ring base, chopstick set, wooden-handled ladle and spatula are included.*

Complete Wok Set Imported by Broadway Hale, Los Angeles, CA. *14-inch diameter, two-quart capacity tempered-steel wok, double handles riveted to base, aluminum dome lid with plastic knob. Wire-mesh skimmer, wooden-handled spatula and ladle, folding steamer rack, chopstick set and ring base are included.*

Chinese Village Kitchen by Taylor & Ng, San Francisco, CA. *14-inch diameter, two-quart capacity wok of tempered steel. Lid has wooden knob. Portable burner has adapter rack that is removed for wok cookery. Wok fits securely into metal supporting rods. Adapter top doubles as a steamer rack. Burner uses denatured alcohol as fuel. Angle-sided ring is included for conventional stove cooking.*

Wooden-Handled Wok by Gourmet Ware, Atlas Metal Spinning™, South San Francisco, CA. *14-inch diameter, two-quart capacity wok of tempered steel. Aluminum dome lid with wooden knob. Wooden handles fastened onto sides with welded-on metal brackets. Angle ring base.*

Double-Handled Wok by Housewares of All Nations, Hoan Products, Ramsey, NJ. *14-inch diameter, two-quart capacity tempered-steel wok with flat aluminum lid. Plastic knob stays cool while cooking. Bowl-shaped handles riveted to base. Straight-sided ring included.*

Wear-Ever® Electric Wok by Wear-Ever Aluminum Co., Chillicothe, OH. *Aluminum, 14-inch diameter, 3-quart capacity. Black non-stick interior, red porcelain exterior. Lid has a plastic knob. Removable heat-control unit.*

Nordic Long-Handled Wok by Nordic Ware®, Northland Aluminum Products, Minneapolis, MN. *Aluminum flat-bottomed wok, 6-quart capacity, 14-inch diameter. Gray non-stick interior. Red-enamel dome lid with plastic knob. Interior has a shelf that holds steamer rack. One metal handle 7½" long, one small metal handle, both attached with rivets.*

Nordic Electric Wok by Nordic Ware®, Northland Aluminum Products, Minneapolis, MN. *Aluminum, 6-quart capacity. 14-inch diameter. Gray non-stick interior. Red-enamel dome lid with platic knob. Interior shelf holds steamer rack. Wok is cradled in black plastic with 2 plastic handles. Removable heat-control unit.*

West Bend® Electric Wok by West Bend Company, West Bend, WI. *Aluminum, 3-quart capacity, 14-inch diameter. Black non-stick interior. Exterior is red enamel with plastic handles. Lid has plastic handle. Wok rests on plastic feet. Removable heat-control unit.*

Wok by Gourmet Products, Newton Highlands, MA. *14-inch diameter, 6-quart capacity. Iron dome lid has clip on one side and plastic handle. Metal side handles. Straight-sided ring included. Set includes steamer, strainer, cleavers and scissors. Chopping board available.*

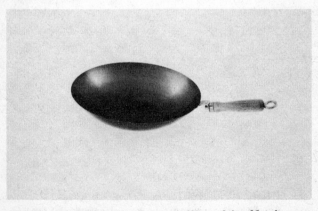

Flat-Bottomed Skillet by Gourmet Ware, Atlas Metal Spinning™, South San Francisco, CA. *14-inch diameter, tempered steel, 2-quart capacity. A single 7-inch wooden handle screws onto welded metal bracket.*

APPETIZERS

Gone are the days when you could get away with cheese dip and a tray of raw vegetables for appetizers. Interest in food has increased tremendously. Party fare should be more substantial and taste really great. Because most households lack a staff of helpers, I've developed hot morsels that can be made ahead and reheated quickly at the crucial moment. They include Egg Roll Appetizers, page 40, Shrimp & Fish Cocktail Croquettes, pages 34 and 35, and deep-fried Cocktail Turnovers, pages 49 through 53.

Cold appetizers can be just as interesting. Pickled Shrimp, page 46, and marinated cold cooked vegetables such as steamed Artichoke Hearts Vinaigrette, page 47, are great. To my mind, a perfect party would include hot appetizers, a cold seafood and one or two cold marinated vegetables. For a really festive appetizer, try my recipe for Chinese Pork in Plum Sauce, page 37.

Have a marvelous time!

THE ORIENTAL TOUCH

Egg-Roll Appetizers, page 40
Curried Pork With Noodles, page 217
Mango Chutney, page 209
Strawberries With Sour Cream &
Brown Sugar

SUMMER DINNER PARTY

Vegetables a la Grecque, page 36
Chicken With Summer Fruit, page 118
Rice Pilaf
Baba au Rhum, page 234

INVITE THE BOSS TO DINNER

Pickled Shrimp, page 46
Braised Veal With Vegetables, page 172
Crusty French Bread
Imperial Ice-Cream Cake, page 252

Salmon Cocktail Croquettes

These little morsels vanish like snow in the sun.

2 large potatoes, (1 lb.), peeled, quartered
Water
2 tablespoons butter
2 tablespoons cream or milk
1/2 teaspoon salt
1 teaspoon paprika
1 teaspoon grated onion
1 (16-oz.) can salmon, drained, boned, flaked
1 egg, slightly beaten with 1 tablespoon water
About 1 cup fine dry bread crumbs
Oil for frying

Place potatoes in a saucepan. Add water to cover and boil until tender. Drain in a colander. Transfer to a bowl. Mash with butter and cream until smooth and fluffy. Add salt, paprika, onion and salmon. Form into small balls. Dip in beaten egg, then roll in crumbs. Chill for 1 hour or longer. Pour oil in wok to 3-inch center depth. Heat to 375°F (191°C). Fry a few croquettes at a time until lightly browned. Drain on paper towel. Makes 8 to 10 croquettes.

Shrimp & Fish Cocktail Croquettes

Something special for seafood lovers.

1-1/2 lbs. fillet of firm white fish
1/2 lb. shrimp, cleaned, deveined
2 tablespoons dry sherry
1 clove garlic, peeled, crushed
1/4 cup butter
1/4 cup all-purpose flour
1 cup milk, heated
1/2 teaspoon salt
1 egg yolk
1/4 cup all-purpose flour
2 eggs, slightly beaten
1 cup fine dry bread crumbs
Oil for deep frying

Place fish fillets and shrimp in a long shallow baking dish. Sprinkle with sherry and garlic. Place on rack in wok over simmering water. Cover loosely with foil. Cover wok. Steam for 10 minutes or until fish flakes easily and shrimp are firm and pink. Remove fish and shrimp. Drain and discard garlic. Finely chop shrimp. Flake fish and combine with shrimp. In a large saucepan, melt butter and stir in 1/4 cup of flour. When blended add heated milk and stir mixture until very thick and smooth. Let cool slightly. Stir in the fish and shrimp. Add salt and egg yolk. Blend and shape into bite-size croquettes. Roll in 1/4 cup flour, dip in beaten egg and then in bread crumbs. Place in a single layer on a tray or baking sheet. Refrigerate for 1 hour or longer. When ready to fry, pour oil in wok to a 3-inch center depth. heat to 375°F (191°C). Lower croquettes 2 or 3 at a time into the hot oil and fry until lightly browned. Drain on paper towel. Makes 8 to 10 servings.

Vegetables a la Grecque

Crisp-tender vegetables in a zesty marinade.

8 very small white onions, peeled
Water
2 small zucchini, trimmed and sliced 1-in. thick
2 small yellow squash, trimmed and sliced 1-in. thick
1 small green or sweet red pepper, cut in narrow strips
1/2 cup oil
1/4 cup dry white wine
2 tablespoons strained lemon juice
1 teaspoon salt
1/2 teaspoon coarse-ground black pepper
1 teaspoon sugar
1 clove garlic, peeled and split lengthwise

In a saucepan, cover onions with water and boil for 15 minutes or until tender; drain. Place onion, zucchini, yellow squash, and green or sweet red pepper in a shallow 10-inch baking dish. Combine oil, wine and lemon juice. Pour over vegetables. Sprinkle with salt, pepper and sugar. Add garlic. Place dish on rack in wok over simmering water. Cover wok and steam vegetables 10 minutes, until they are crisp-tender. Remove dish from wok. Cook at room temperature. Cover with foil or plastic wrap and refrigerate for several hours or overnight. With a slotted spoon remove vegetables from marinade. Arrange on a large round platter: white onions in the center, zucchini and yellow squash in a circle around them, and green or red pepper strips around the edge of the plate. Serve with cocktail picks. Makes 6 to 8 servings.

Chinese Pork in Plum Sauce

Sliced wafer-thin, this is a sensational appetizer.

1-1/2 to 2 lbs. center-cut fillet of pork
1/2 cup plum jam
1/2 cup sherry
1/4 cup lemon juice
1/4 cup soy sauce
1 clove garlic, peeled, crushed
1 (1-in.) cube fresh ginger, crushed

Place pork in a small baking dish just large enough to hold it. In a small saucepan, combine plum jam with sherry, lemon juice and soy sauce. Cook over low heat until jam is melted. Pour over pork. Add garlic and ginger. Cover and refrigerate 12 to 24 hours. Place dish on rack in wok over simmering water. Cook loosely with foil. Cover wok. Let meat steam in marinade for 1 to 1-1/2 hours or until tender. Baste and turn meat in marinade several times during cooking. Let meat cool in marinade. Drain. Slice very thin and serve at room temperature with leftover marinade. Makes 10 to 12 servings.

Variation:

Use meat for a stir-fry dish. Mince and use as a filling in egg rolls or steamed dumplings.

Cocktail Won Ton

Delicious little Chinese dumplings usually added to Won Ton Soup, but they make a fun appetizer without the soup.

1-1/2 cup finely minced cooked pork
3 tablespoons finely minced celery
2 tablespoons chili sauce
2 or 3 drops Tabasco® sauce
2 tablespoons sherry
1 (7-1/2-oz.) can green chilies
24 won ton skins, frozen, thawed
2 cups chicken broth

In a small bowl, combine pork, celery, chili sauce, Tabasco® sauce, sherry and green chilies. Mix to a smooth paste. Spread won ton skins out on large chopping board. Place a teaspoon of filling in center of each. Bring each corner of won ton skin up and moisten edges with fingers to seal seams, making a pouch. The 4 seams will be on one side. Pour broth in a shallow baking dish. Place 12 won ton at a time seam side down in dish. Place on rack in wok over simmering water. Cover wok and steam for 30 minutes. Remove with slotted spoon to a heated platter and keep warm. Serve hot or at room temperature. Makes 24 won ton appetizers.

Variation:

Won ton can be prepared ahead, frozen and reheated by steaming in your wok.

Chicken Filling for Won Ton

Elegant flavor!

1-1/2 cups finely minced cooked chicken
2 tablespoons finely minced celery
2 tablespoons finely minced chutney
1 tablespoon sherry

Combine filling ingredients and blend well. See instructions for filling won ton above. Makes filling for 24 won ton.

Sausage Filling for Won Ton

Hot and peppery!

1 cup cooked ground sausage
3 tablespoons finely minced celery
3 tablespoons finely minced green pepper
1 medium apple, peeled, grated
1 (7-1/2-oz.) can chopped green chilies, drained
3 tablespoons chili sauce

Combine filling ingredients and blend well. See instructions for filling won ton above. Makes filling for 24 won ton.

Egg Roll Appetizers

Crisp, tasty delicacies.

14 to 20 frozen egg-roll wrappers
Egg-Roll Filling, see following recipes
Oil for deep frying
Mustard

Thaw egg-roll wrappers until pliable. Use about 1/4 cup filling. Place filling diagonally across the center of a wrapper. Lift the lower triangle of wrapper over the filling and tuck the point under it, leaving the upper point of the wrapper flat. Bring the 2 end flaps up and over the enclosed filling. Press flaps down firmly. Dip your fingers in cold water and brush them over the upper exposed triangle of dough. Then roll the filled portion over it until you have a neat package. Cold water seals the edges and keeps the package intact. Cover the filled egg roll with a clean, dry towel until ready to fry. Fill wok with oil to 3-inch center depth. Heat to 375°F (191°C). With tongs lower 4 or 5 egg rolls into the hot fat. Fry for 3 to 4 minutes, or until golden brown and crisp. Drain on a double thickness of paper towels. Cut across into 2 or 3 slices. Serve warm. If desired, serve with dips such as hot mustard, plum sauce or soy sauce. Makes 18 to 20 filled egg rolls.

Variation:

If you are not going to fry egg rolls within about 30 minutes, cover them with plastic wrap and store in the refrigerator or freezer.

How to Make Egg-Roll Appetizers

Dice and chop the filling ingredients.

Place about 1/4 cup of cooled filling diagonally across the center of the egg-roll wrapper. Fold one corner over the filling.

Moisten with cold water. Fold over the two end corners. Roll the filled portion over to form a package. Press down firmly on the seams to seal the wrappers.

Deep-fry the egg rolls in hot oil 3 to 4 minutes, turning once. Remove from the wok when they are golden brown.

Shrimp Egg-Roll Filling

A seafood treat in a crisp egg roll.

1/2 lb. raw shrimp, cleaned, deveined
1 teaspoon sherry
1 teaspoon salt
1/2 teaspoon cornstarch
3 tablespoons oil
2 cups finely diced celery
1/2 teaspoon sugar
1 tablespoon water
1/2 cup fresh bean sprouts, if desired
1 cup shredded lettuce
1 cup finely chopped water chestnuts

Combine shrimp, sherry, salt and cornstarch in a small non-metal bowl. Let stand about 15 minutes. Heat 1 tablespoon oil in wok. Add shrimp mixture and stir-fry until shrimp are firm and pink. Spoon contents of wok into a mixing bowl. Add remaining oil to wok. Add celery, stir-fry about 2 to 3 minutes. Add sugar and water. Cover and steam for 1 minute. Uncover, and stir-fry until liquid evaporates. Add to shrimp mixture. Add remaining ingredients and blend. Cool before using. Makes filling for 14 to 16 egg rolls.

Chicken Egg-Roll Filling

Mushrooms and Chinese vegetables combine for delicate flavor and texture.

1 lb. boneless chicken breasts, finely chopped
2 tablespoons cornstarch
2 tablespoons soy sauce
1 teaspoon ginger
4 tablespoons oil
1/4 lb. mushrooms, finely chopped
1/2 cup finely chopped bamboo shoots
1 small cabbage, finely chopped, about 3 cups
1/4 cup finely chopped water chestnuts
1 teaspoon salt
2 teaspoons sugar

In a small mixing bowl combine chicken, cornstarch, soy sauce and ginger. Blend; let stand for 15 minutes. Heat oil in wok. Stir-fry mushrooms about 1 minute. Add chicken and continue to stir-fry until firm and white. Add remaining ingredients and stir-fry until cabbage is crisp-tender. Cool before filling egg-roll wrappers. Makes filling for 20 egg rolls.

Shrimp & Pork Egg-Roll Filling

Everyone's favorite.

2 tablespoons oil
3 cups finely chopped celery
1/2 cup finely chopped mushrooms
1/2 lb. raw shrimp, cleaned, deveined, finely chopped
1 cup finely chopped bean sprouts
1 cup finely chopped lean cooked pork
1 tablespoon soy sauce
1 tablespoon sherry
1 teaspoon salt
1 teaspoon sugar
1 tablespoon cornstarch dissolved in
   2 tablespoons water

Heat oil in wok. Add celery and mushrooms. Stir-fry about 1 minute. Add shrimp. Continue to stir-fry until shrimp are firm and pink. Add bean sprouts and pork. Stir to blend. Stir in soy sauce, sherry, salt, sugar and dissolved cornstarch. Remove from heat and cool before using. Makes filling for 18 to 20 egg rolls.

Pickled Shrimp

These vanish almost as soon as they are served.

1-1/2 lbs. shrimp, cleaned, deveined, thawed if frozen
Juice of 1 lemon
2 tablespoons soy sauce
2 tablespoons chopped green onion
1 tablespoon peeled, chopped fresh ginger

Place shrimp in a shallow baking dish. Mix lemon juice and soy sauce. Pour over shrimp. Sprinkle with green onion and ginger. Place dish on rack in wok over simmering water. Cover wok and steam for 5 to 10 minutes or until shrimp are pink. Remove and cool. Cover dish with plastic wrap or foil. Refrigerate shrimp in cooking marinade for 4 to 6 hours. Drain and serve cold. Use cocktail picks for serving. Makes about 18 to 20 shrimp, depending on size of shrimp.

Escabeche

Piquant fish strips to serve icy cold.

1 tablespoon oil
1 teaspoon salt
1 mild purple onion, peeled, sliced thin
3 tablespoons oil
2 lbs. halibut or sole fillets, cut into 1-1/2 to 2-in. slices
1/4 cup tarragon or other flavorful vinegar
1/2 cup salad oil

2 tablespoons strained lemon juice
1 teaspoon salt
1/2 teaspoon pepper
1 clove garlic, peeled
Lettuce leaves
8 to 10 pimiento-stuffed olives, sliced

Heat 1 tablespoon of oil with 1/4 teaspoon salt in wok over moderate heat. Add onion and cook, stirring until soft. Spoon into a long shallow baking dish and set aside. Add about 1 tablespoon of oil to wok. Over high heat cook a few fish slices at a time until they are firm and white. Add oil as needed until fish is cooked. Add to onions. Combine vinegar, oil and lemon juice. Pour over fish and onions. Sprinkle with salt and pepper. Add garlic. Cover and refrigerate. Chill 12 to 24 hours before serving. Drain. Remove and discard garlic. Arrange fish on crisp lettuce leaves and sprinkle with olive slices. Makes 6 to 8 servings.

Artichoke Hearts Vinaigrette

A touch of elegance.

1 (9-oz.) pkg. frozen artichoke hearts
2 tablespoons cider vinegar
1 clove garlic, peeled, crushed
1/2 teaspoon salt
1 tablespoon sugar
1/8 teaspoon pepper
1/2 cup salad oil

Place frozen artichoke hearts in a shallow baking dish. Combine remaining ingredients. Pour over and around artichoke hearts. Place dish on rack in wok over simmering water. Cover wok and steam for about 15 minutes or until artichoke hearts are heated but still firm. Remove from wok. Cool and refrigerate for several hours in cooking liquid. Drain just before serving. Serve on cocktail picks. Makes 6 to 8 servings.

Brussels Sprouts With Anchovies

Anchovy lovers will unite around this one.

1 (10-oz.) pkg. frozen Brussels sprouts
1 (2-oz.) can anchovy fillets in oil
2 tablespoons lemon juice
2 tablespoons oil
1 clove garlic, peeled crushed
1 (1-in.) cube fresh ginger, crushed

Place frozen Brussels sprouts in a shallow baking dish. Drain anchovy fillets and reserve all oil. Combine oil from drained anchovy fillets with lemon juice and oil. Pour mixture over Brussels sprouts. Add garlic and ginger to liquid. Place dish on rack in wok over simmering water. Cover wok and steam about 15 minutes, until Brussels sprouts are cooked but slightly crisp. Cool, refrigerate for several hours. Drain just before serving. Wrap one anchovy fillet around each Brussels sprout and secure with a toothpick. Makes 6 to 8 servings.

Cocktail Turnovers

Bite-size appetizers made with frozen patty shells.

4 frozen patty shells
Filling for Turnovers, see following recipes
Oil for deep-frying

Thaw patty shells until soft but still cold. On a lightly floured board roll one shell into an 8-1/2- to 9-inch circle. Trim edges to make an 8-inch square. Cut each square in 4 small (4-inch) squares. Turn each toward you to form a diamond. Place a small amount of filling on the side nearest you. Fold pastry over to form a triangle. Seal edges with water and press together with fork tines. Place turnovers on an ungreased baking sheet, not touching. Place in freezer until firm. When ready to fry, fill wok with oil to a 3-inch center depth. Heat to 375°F (191°C). Fry frozen turnovers in hot oil until nicely browned on both sides. Drain on paper towel. Serve warm or at room temperature. Fried turnovers may be made ahead then reheated in a 375°F (191°C) oven. Makes 16 small turnovers.

Shrimp Filling for Turnovers

Memories of the Orient Express.

1/4 lb. shrimp, cleaned, deveined and finely minced
3 water chestnuts, finely minced
1 tablespoon chutney, finely minced
2 tablespoons mayonnaise

Combine all ingredients. Mix to a paste. Refrigerate for several hours to allow flavors to mellow. Makes filling for 16 turnovers.

Chicken Filling for Turnovers

Appeals to exotic tastes.

1/2 cup finely minced cooked chicken
2 tablespoons finely minced celery
3 tablespoons mayonnaise
1/2 teaspoon curry powder
1/2 teaspoon currant jelly

Combine all ingredients. Mix to a paste. Refrigerate for several hours to allow flavors to mellow. Makes filling for 16 turnovers.

Pork Filling for Turnovers

Fit for a Hawaiian luau.

1/2 cup finely minced lean cooked pork
5 water chestnuts finely minced
2 tablespoons thick steak sauce
2 tablespoons pineapple juice

Combine all ingredients. Mix to a paste. Refrigerate for several hours to allow flavors to mellow. Makes filling for 16 turnovers.

Bacon Filling for Turnovers

Here's a sandwich turnover!

1/2 cup crumbled crisp cooked bacon
1/4 cup finely shredded lettuce
2 tablespoons mayonnaise
1 tablespoon grated sharp cheese

Combine all ingredients. Mix to a paste. Refrigerate for several hours to allow flavors to mellow. Makes filling for 16 turnovers.

Beef Filling for Turnovers

Strong, hearty flavor.

1/2 cup finely minced cooked beef
1/4 cup finely minced onion
2 tablespoons thick steak sauce
1 tablespoon Worcestershire sauce

Combine all ingredients. Mix to a paste. Refrigerate for several hours to allow flavors to mellow. Makes filling for 16 turnovers.

Cheese Filling for Turnovers

Indescribably delicious!

1/2 cup grated sharp cheese
2 tablespoons cream cheese, softened
3 tablespoons sour cream
1 teaspoon Tabasco® sauce

Combine all ingredients. Mix to a paste. Refrigerate for several hours to allow flavors to mellow. Makes filling for 16 turnovers.

Chicken-Liver Filling for Turnovers

The epitome of sophistication!

1/2 cup cooked chicken livers, mashed to a smooth
   paste
1/4 cup finely minced celery
2 teaspoons currant jelly
1 tablespoon mayonnaise
2 tablespoons dry sherry

Combine all ingredients. Mix to a paste. Refrigerate for
several hours to allow flavors to mellow. Makes filling for
16 turnovers.

VEGETABLES & RICE

A lot of otherwise good cooks are baffled by vegetable cookery. No matter how carefully prepared, the results are often disappointing. Because of this, too many people eat vegetables, not as a pleasure, but as a duty. The incredible wok produces delicious, tender-crisp vegetables with all the flavor of a sunny garden. Whether stir-fried, steamed or deep-fried, every vegetable from asparagus to zucchini looks and tastes glorious. If you think steamed vegetables are dull, try the Three-Star Vegetable Platter on page 60. If spinach seems an unlikely choice for a party meal, wait until you have tasted Spinach Stir-Fry, page 62. It's a far cry from the watery, tasteless limp fare cooked in an ordinary pot.

Does your family leave lettuce untouched on their plates and regard parsley only as a decoration? If so try my stir-fry recipes which use shredded lettuce and minced parsley as ingredients. I promise you they are delicious.

Fresh corn retains its just-cooked flavor when it's wok steamed; none of its goodness is poured down the drain with the cooking water. And asparagus! Surely nothing is more delicious than this first delicacy of spring when cooked in your wok. Wok cookery brings out vegetables' best texture and taste. Try combining fresh with frozen for delicious results. It's so easy, quick and so downright good.

To prepare fresh greens for wok cookery: Wash thoroughly, place them in your sink and cover with cold water. Swish them around a bit. All the sand and dirt will sink to the bottom while the clean greens float to the top. Lift out onto paper towels. Then roll loosely in paper towels and place in the crisping compartment of your refrigerator. In a few hours they will be bone-dry and crisper than when you brought them home.

All other vegetables should be trimmed, washed, dried and peeled if necessary. Then care should be taken to chop, mince or slice them to perfection. These few minutes of preparation are made up in the double-quick cooking time.

TEXAS STYLE

Texas Barbecued Braised Beef, page 158
Mexican Rice, page 66
Cucumber & Tomato Salad
Marmalade Pudding Cake, page 255

TODAY'S CATCH IS SHRIMP

Sweet & Sour Shrimp, page 128
Oriental Rice, page 60
Winter-Fruit Compote au Kirsch, page 259

VEGETABLE DINNER

Three-Star Vegetable Platter, page 60
Buttered Crusty Rolls
Mocha Sponge Cake, page 265

Paprika Rice

A lovely rice pilaf to go with chicken.

1 cup long-grain rice
Water
1 tablespoon oil
1/2 teaspoon salt
1 cup chicken broth, heated
1 cup water
1 teaspoon Hungarian paprika
1/4 teaspoon pepper

Place rice in a bowl and cover with cold water. Let stand 30 minutes, then drain in a colander. Heat oil with salt in wok. Add rice and cook, stirring until grains are coated with oil. Pour in heated broth and water. Add paprika and pepper. Stir to blend. Bring to a full boil. Cover, lower heat and simmer for 12 to 15 minutes or until rice is tender and almost all liquid has been absorbed. Remove wok from heat and let stand, covered, for 10 to 12 minutes or until all liquid has been absorbed. Makes 4 to 6 servings.

Italian Rice Ring

Fill this flavorful rice ring with a medley of vegetables for a beautiful buffet dish.

4 tablespoons butter
1/4 cup finely minced onion
1-1/2 cups long-grain rice

1 cup chicken broth
2 cups water
1 cup grated Parmesan cheese
Salt to taste

Butter a 6-cup ring mold. Melt butter in wok over low heat. Add onion and stir until soft. Add rice and stir until rice is coated with butter and has turned light yellow. Add broth and water. Bring to a boil, stirring occasionally. Lower heat. Cover and simmer until rice is tender and almost all liquid has been absorbed. Remove wok from heat and let stand, covered, until all liquid is absorbed. Stir in cheese. Season to taste with salt. Turn into buttered ring mold and press rice down gently. Turn onto a serving plate or keep warm until ready to serve. Makes 6 to 8 servings.

Curried Fried Rice

A delightful blend of tastes and textures.

2 tablespoons oil
1/2 teaspoon salt
1 clove garlic, peeled, crushed
3 cups cold cooked rice
2 eggs
1 teaspoon curry powder
1 cup cooked green peas
1/2 cup chopped dry-roasted peanuts, for garnish
1/4 cup minced chives or green onions, for garnish
Mango Chutney, page 209, if desired

Heat oil with salt in wok. Add garlic and stir against sides of wok until browned. Remove and discard garlic. Add rice and stir until grains are coated with oil. In a small bowl, beat eggs with curry powder. Pour over rice and stir-fry until set. Add peas and stir gently until heated. Sprinkle with chopped peanuts and green onions. Serve with Mango Chutney, if desired. Makes 4 to 6 servings.

Cannellini Stir-Fry

A fantastic vegetable medley!

3 slices bacon, chopped
1 clove garlic, peeled, minced
1 large mild onion, peeled, and finely minced
1 cup finely chopped cabbage
1 medium zucchini, trimmed and finely chopped
1 large tomato, chopped
1/4 cup water
1/4 teaspoon mixed Italian herbs
1/2 teaspoon salt
1/4 teaspoon pepper
1 (20-oz.) can Cannellini (white kidney beans)
1/4 cup grated Parmesan cheese
Grated Parmesan cheese, if desired

Place bacon in wok and stir-fry over medium heat until fat is rendered and bacon is crisp. Remove bacon, crumble and reserve. Pour off all but 2 tablespoons fat. Add garlic and onion. Stir-fry until tender. Add cabbage, zucchini, tomato, water, Italian herbs, salt and pepper. Stir to mix. Cover and steam. Stir occasionally until vegetables are still slightly crisp. Add beans and stir until heated. Stir in cheese and top with crumbled bacon. Serve with additional cheese, if desired. Makes 4 servings.

Fried Rice With Bacon, Lettuce & Tomato

Bacon, lettuce & tomato on rice? Why not?

6 slices thick-sliced bacon
1/4 cup chopped onion
1 tablespoon sherry
2 tablespoons chicken broth
3 cups cold cooked rice
1 cup shredded lettuce
1 tomato, cut in strips, pulp and seeds removed
1 teaspoon Worcestershire sauce

Place bacon in wok over very low heat. Cook until crisp, about 30 minutes. Remove bacon, drain on paper towel and crumble. Pour all but 2 tablespoons rendered fat from wok. Increase heat to medium. Add onion and stir-fry about 1 minute. Add sherry and chicken broth. Place cooked rice on top. Cover and steam for 30 seconds. Uncover and stir-fry until rice is hot. Stir in lettuce, tomato strips and crumbled bacon. Sprinkle with Worcestershire sauce. Stir-fry until well blended. Makes 6 servings.

Oriental Rice

A fabulous way to use leftover rice.

1 tablespoon oil
2 cups cold cooked rice
1/2 cup chopped water chestnuts
1/2 cup seedless raisins
1/4 cup soy sauce

Heat oil in wok. Add cooked rice and cook, stirring and tossing gently until grains are coated with oil. Add water chestnuts and raisins. Continue stir-tossing until mixture is heated. Add soy sauce and blend. Makes 4 to 6 servings.

Variation:

Stir diced cooked meat or chicken into the rice with the water chestnuts and raisins.

Three-Star Vegetable Platter

Tasty stuffed tomatoes surrounded by zucchini and corn on the cob.

4 medium tomatoes
1 tablespoon oil
1 clove garlic, finely minced
2 tablespoons finely minced onion
2 tablespoons finely minced green pepper
1 cup corn-bread-stuffing mix
2 tablespoons chutney, finely minced

1/4 cup chicken broth
1/4 cup water
1/4 teaspoon salt
1/4 teaspoon black pepper
4 small zucchini
4 ears fresh corn, cleaned

Cut stem ends from tomatoes. Carefully scoop out pulp into a small bowl. Reserve shells. Heat oil in wok. Stir-fry garlic, onion and green pepper until soft. Stir in tomato pulp, stuffing mix, chutney, broth, water, salt and pepper. Stir-fry about 3 minutes over low heat. Chop tomato pieces as they cook. Fill tomato shells with mixture. Fill wok with water to bottom of steaming rack. Bring to a simmer. Wash zucchini and place in one end of a shallow baking dish. Place on rack in wok over simmering water. Cover and steam 15 minutes. Uncover and add stuffed tomatoes to dish. Place 2 ears of corn directly on rack at each side of dish. Cover. Steam all vegetables 15 to 20 minutes or until zucchini is tender. Serve hot. Makes 4 servings.

American Vegetable Stir-Fry

Serve for a quick and tasty lunch with sliced cold meat.

2 tablespoons oil
1 teaspoon salt
1 clove garlic, peeled, crushed
1 onion, peeled, chopped
2 carrots, peeled, sliced thin at a 45-degree angle

1 small white turnip, peeled, sliced thin, slices cut
  in quarters
1/2 cup thinly sliced celery
1 (10-oz.) pkg. frozen green peas, thawed
1/4 cup chicken broth
2 tablespoons Sweet & Sour Sauce, page 126

Heat oil with salt in wok. Add garlic and stir against sides of
wok until lightly browned. Remove and discard garlic. Add
onion, carrots, turnip, celery and peas. Stir-fry 1 minute
over high heat. Pour in broth. Cover, and simmer for 5
minutes. Uncover and stir-fry unti liquid evaporates. Stir in
Sweet & Sour Sauce. Makes 4 servings.

Spinach Stir-Fry

Even children love stir-fried spinach.

2 tablespoons oil
1 teaspoon salt
1 clove garlic
1 (10-oz.) pkg. frozen spinach, thawed
1 teaspoon sugar
1 teaspoon apple-cider vinegar
1 teaspoon cornstarch dissolved in 1 tablespoon water

Heat oil with salt in wok. Add garlic and stir against sides of
wok until lightly browned. Remove and discard garlic. Add
spinach and stir-fry about 30 seconds. Sprinkle with sugar
and vinegar. Add dissolved cornstarch. Stir to blend. Cover
and steam 30 seconds. Uncover and stir-fry about 30
seconds. Makes 3 to 4 servings.

Sicilian Stuffed Artichokes

Dress up artichokes for a special dinner.

1-1/2 cups soft bread crumbs
1/2 cup chicken broth
1 small onion, peeled, minced
1 clove garlic, peeled, minced
1 (2-oz.) can anchovy fillets in oil
1/4 cup grated Parmesan cheese
4 large artichokes

Combine bread crumbs, broth, onion and garlic. Chop anchovies and add with anchovy oil to bread crumb mixture. Stir in cheese. Set aside. Cut off each artichoke stem, leaving bottom flat so the artichoke will sit upright. Place each on its side on a chopping board. Cut off tips with a sharp cleaver or kitchen scissors. Place artichokes on rack in wok over simmering water. Cover and steam for 30 minutes. Remove from wok. Let cool slightly. Remove choke by gently separating the leaves and scraping out the spiny center with a spoon. Stuff the leaves and center of each artichoke with stuffing mixture. Place in a baking dish just large enough to hold them upright. Place dish on rack in wok. Steam for 30 minutes or until artichokes are tender and leaves can be pulled off easily. Makes 4 servings.

Zucchini Italian-Style

Make the most of summer's fresh zucchini with tomatoes and cheese.

2 tablespoons oil
1/2 cup chopped onion
4 medium zucchini, trimmed, coarsely chopped
1 (1-lb.) can stewed tomatoes
1/4 teaspoon mixed Italian herbs
1/2 teaspoon salt
1/4 teaspoon coarse-ground black pepper
1/3 cup grated Parmesan cheese

Heat oil in wok. Add onion and zucchini. Stir-fry about 1 minute. Add tomatoes, Italian herbs, salt and pepper. Bring to a boil. Cover and steam 4 to 5 minutes or until zucchini is still slightly crisp. Stir in cheese and stir-fry about 30 seconds. Makes 4 to 6 servings.

Mandarin Cauliflower & Broccoli

Everyone will love these vegetables.

2 tablespoons oil
1/2 teaspoon salt
10 small mushrooms, sliced lengthwise through stems
1 small onion, peeled, minced
1 cup water
1-1/2 cups bite-size cauliflower pieces
1-1/2 cups bite-size broccoli pieces (stems and flowerets)

1/2 cup water
2 teaspoons sugar
2 teaspoons cornstarch dissolved in 1 tablespoon water

Heat oil with salt in wok. Add mushrooms and onion. Stir-fry about 2 minutes or until tender. Pour in water and bring to a boil. Stir in cauliflower. Cover and steam for 5 minutes. Add broccoli and mix well. Cover and steam 10 minutes, stirring occasionally. Add remaining water and sugar. Bring to a simmer. Stir in dissolved cornstarch. Stir until sauce thickens and vegetables are well coated. Makes 4 servings.

Asparagus Stir-Fry

One minute is all you need to cook.

1 (10-oz.) pkg. frozen asparagus, thawed
1 tablespoon oil
1 teaspoon salt
1 tablespoon water
1/4 teaspoon sugar
1 tablespoon lemon juice
Pimiento strips, for garnish

Cut off asparagus tips. Slice stalks diagonally into thin strips. Heat oil with salt in wok over high heat. Add asparagus and stir-fry about 30 seconds. Add water, cover and steam for 30 seconds. Uncover, sprinkle with sugar and lemon juice. Stir-fry about 30 seconds. Garnish with pimiento strips. Makes 3 to 4 servings.

Mexican Rice

A great accompaniment to a Mexican feast.

2 tablespoons oil
1 teaspoon salt
1 cup long-grain rice
1/2 cup finely chopped onion
1 clove garlic, peeled, minced
1 medium tomato, peeled, seeded and finely chopped
1 teaspoon chili powder
1 cup chicken broth
1-1/2 cups water
1 tablespoon chopped parsley

Heat oil with salt in wok. Add rice. Stir-fry over medium heat until rice is coated with oil and has turned light yellow. Add onion and garlic, stir-frying until onion is tender. Add tomato and chili powder. Cook, stirring until tomato is soft. Add chicken broth and water. Bring to a boil, stirring. Cover and reduce heat. Simmer until almost all liquid is absorbed and rice is tender. Remove wok from heat and let rice stand, covered, for about 10 minutes or until all liquid is absorbed. Gently stir in parsley with a fork. Makes 6 servings.

Olive & Almond Rice Casserole

Perfect for a festive luncheon.

1 tablespoon oil
1/2 cup slivered almonds
1/4 cup finely minced green onion
1/4 cup finely minced parsley
2 cups cooked rice
1/2 cup chicken broth
3 eggs, slightly beaten
1/4 cup sliced pimiento-stuffed olives
1/4 cup grated mild Swiss cheese
Paprika, for garnish

Heat oil in wok. Add almonds, green onion and parsley. Stir-fry until almonds are golden. Add cooked rice and toss to blend. Pour in broth. Remove wok from heat. Cover and let stand until slightly cooled. Stir in eggs, olives and cheese. Mix well. Spoon into a 1-quart casserole dish. Place dish on rack in wok over simmering water. Cover wok and steam for 30 minutes. Sprinkle with paprika and serve from the dish. Makes 4 to 6 servings.

Main-Course Succotash With Noodles

Try this spicy dish for an economical treat.

1/2 lb. spicy sausage meat
1 small onion, peeled, chopped
1/2 small green pepper, seeded, chopped
1 (1-lb.) can tomatoes
1 (10-oz.) pkg. frozen succotash, thawed
1/2 teaspoon salt
1/4 teaspoon pepper
1 (8-oz.) pkg. flat noodles, cooked
1/2 cup grated sharp Cheddar cheese

Stir-fry sausage meat in wok, over medium heat until no longer pink. Add onion and green pepper. Continue to stir until vegetables are tender. With a large spoon remove all rendered fat. Add tomatoes and succotash. Cook, stirring and breaking vegetables apart. Add salt and pepper. Cover and steam, stirring occasionally until beans and corn are tender. Add noodles and cheese. Stir until heated. Makes 4 to 6 servings.

Broccoli Stir-Fry

A delightful way to cook this green vegetable.

1 (10-oz.) pkg. frozen broccoli, thawed
1 tablespoon oil
1 (1-in.) cube fresh ginger, peeled
1 clove garlic, peeled, crushed
1/2 teaspoon salt
2 tablespoons water, more if needed
1/2 teaspoon sugar
1 teaspoon grated lemon peel

Break off flowerets from thawed broccoli. Cut each into 3 or 4 pieces. Trim and cut stems into thin strips. Heat oil in wok. Add ginger, garlic and salt. Stir-fry about 1 minute over high heat. Remove and discard ginger and garlic. Add broccoli stems. Stir-fry about 30 seconds. Add water. Cover and steam for 2 minutes. Add flowerets, sugar and grated lemon peel. Stir-fry about 30 seconds. Cover. Steam for 1 minute or until broccoli is tender. Add a little more water if needed. Makes 3 to 4 servings.

New-Style Southern String Beans

Traditionally served with steamed new potatoes.

2 slices bacon, chopped
1 clove garlic, peeled, crushed
1 lb. green beans, ends trimmed
1/2 cup water or chicken broth

easpoon sugar
alt and pepper to taste

Cook bacon in wok over moderate heat until crisp.
Remove and drain on paper towel. Pour off all but 1
tablespoon bacon fat. Turn heat to high. Add garlic and stir
against sides of wok until lightly browned. Remove and
discard garlic. Add beans to wok and stir-fry about 1
minute. Add water or broth. Cover and simmer for 10
minutes, until beans are still slightly crisp. Add sugar and
stir-fry, uncovered, until liquid has evaporated. Stir in
crumbled bacon. Season with salt and pepper to taste.
Makes 4 servings.

Potatoes Provençale

Great served with cold meat and tomatoes vinaigrette.

2 tablespoons oil
1/4 teaspoon salt
1 clove garlic, finely minced
6 boiled potatoes, peeled, diced
1/2 cup finely minced parsley
1 tablespoon Sauce Diable or
    1 teaspoon Worcestershire sauce and
    1 teaspoon mustard

Heat oil in wok with salt over high heat. Add garlic and
stir-fry about 30 seconds. Add potatoes. Lower heat to
moderate and stir-fry until heated and flecked with brown.
Stir in parsley and Sauce Diable or Worcestershire sauce
with mustard. Makes 6 servings.

Mushrooms With Noodles

Mushrooms add class to noodles and stuffing mix.

1 (12-oz.) pkg. flat noodles
Salt
Water
A few drops oil
3 tablespoons oil
1/2 lb. mushrooms, trimmed, sliced thin lengthwise
   through stems
1/2 teaspoon salt
1/4 teaspoon coarse-ground black pepper
1 cup beef broth
1 tablespoon soy sauce
1 teaspoon cornstarch dissolved in 2 tablespoons water
1 cup herb-flavored stuffing mix
1/4 cup finely minced parsley

Drop noodles into a large pot of rapidly boiling salted water. Add a few drops of oil. Cook until noodles rise to the surface and are pliable, about 1 minute. Drain, place in a large bowl and toss with 1 tablespoon of the oil. Heat remaining 2 tablespoons oil in wok. Add mushrooms and stir-fry about 1 minute. Add salt, pepper and broth. Cover and steam for 1 minute. Add soy sauce and stir in dissolved cornstarch. Add stuffing mix and noodles. Stir and toss until heated and noodles are tender. Stir in parsley. Makes 6 servings.

Potatoes O'Brien

Hearty and satisfying.

3 tablespoons oil
1 teaspoon salt
1/2 cup chopped onion
1/2 cup chopped green pepper
1/2 cup chopped pimientos, drained
4 medium potatoes, peeled, finely diced
1/4 cup beef broth, more if needed
1/2 teaspoon Worcestershire sauce

Heat oil with salt in wok. Add onion, green pepper, pimiento and potatoes. Stir-fry over medium heat about 3 to 4 minutes. Combine broth with Worcestershire sauce and pour over vegetables and potatoes. Cover and steam for 10 minutes. Stir occasionally. Add a little more broth if potatoes become dry. Uncover and stir-fry until liquid is absorbed. Makes 4 to 6 servings.

How to Make Potatoes O'Brien

These are the vegetables you will need to make Potatoes O'Brien.

Dice the potatoes and combine with chopped onion, chopped green pepper and chopped pimientos.

Stir-fry over medium heat 3 to 4 minutes before adding broth and Worcestershire sauce.

Rice & Sausage Mexican Style

Hot, spicy & colorful.

1 lb. country-style sausage
1/2 cup minced onion
1 medium green pepper, chopped
1 tablespoon chili powder
3 cups chicken broth
1 cup long-grain converted rice
1 (8-oz.) can tomato sauce
Salt to taste
1 large avocado, peeled, seeded, sliced, and sprinkled
   with lemon juice, for garnish
Pimiento strips, for garnish

Heat wok. Add sausage and stir-fry over medium heat until no longer pink. Add onion and pepper. Continue stirring until onion and pepper are soft. Spoon off and discard rendered fat. Stir in chili powder and add broth. Bring to a boil and add rice. Cover and cook, stirring often for 15 minutes. Stir in tomato sauce. Cover wok and simmer until all liquid has been absorbed. Season with salt to taste. Spoon onto serving plates and garnish with avocado and pimiento. Makes 4 servings.

Wok-Top Vegetables & Stuffing Mix

Hearty appetites really go for this!

2 tablespoons soy sauce
1 tablespoon catsup
2 tablespoons sherry
1 teaspoon sugar
1/2 cup water
2 teaspoons cornstarch
2 tablespoons oil
6 small yellow squash, trimmed, coarsely chopped
1 small white onion, peeled, chopped
1 small carrot, peeled, cut in 1-in. slices, cut lengthwise
 into "matchsticks"
About 4 tablespoons water
1/4 cup minced parsley
1/2 cup bean sprouts
1/2 cup herb-flavored chicken stuffing mix

In a small bowl, combine soy sauce, catsup, sherry, sugar and water. Stir in cornstarch. Set aside. Heat oil in wok. Add squash, onion and carrot. Stir-fry over high heat about 1 minute. Add about 2 tablespoons of water. Cover and steam about 30 seconds. Uncover and repeat stir-frying and steaming, adding remaining water, until vegetables are crisp-tender. Stir in parsley and bean sprouts. Add soy-sauce-catsup mixture. When bubbly hot add stuffing mix. Blend and serve. Makes 4 to 6 servings.

Tomato Curry

Serve this spicy curry with sliced cold meat for an interesting & easy supper.

2 tablespoons oil
1/2 cup chopped onion
1 tart apple, peeled, cored and chopped
2 teaspoons curry powder, or to taste
3/4 cup water
4 large ripe tomatoes, chopped
1 teaspoon vinegar
1 teaspoon sugar
1/2 cup herb-seasoned stuffing mix

Heat oil in wok. Add onion and apple. Stir-fry until onion is soft. Stir in curry powder. Add water. Cover and steam for 2 minutes. Add tomatoes and stir-fry until soft. Cover and steam for 2 minutes or until tomatoes have given off some of their liquid. Add sugar and stuffing mix. Stir-fry about 1 minute. Makes 4 to 6 servings.

Corn Timbales With Ham & Asparagus

A tasty one-dish lunch.

2 eggs
1/2 cup milk
1 tablespoon grated Parmesan cheese
1/2 cup whole-kernel corn

1 tablespoon chopped pimiento, drained
2 slices lean cooked ham, cut in rounds
1 (10-oz.) pkg. frozen asparagus, thawed
1 tablespoon butter, cut in slivers
1 tablespoon lemon juice
Salt to taste

Lightly butter two 1/2-cup timbale molds or custard cups. Beat eggs with milk until blended. Stir in cheese, corn and pimiento. Pour into buttered timbale molds or custard cups. Place in baking dish, on rack over simmering water in wok. Cover dish loosely with foil. Cover wok and steam for 20 minutes. Place ham slices and asparagus on baking dish. Continue to steam for 10 minutes. Remove ham and place each slice on a serving plate. Unmold timbales over ham. Dot asparagus with butter and sprinkle with lemon juice and salt to taste. Steam until butter melts. Arrange asparagus on each plate with ham and timbales. Pour melted butter and lemon juice over asparagus. Serve at once. Makes 2 servings.

Eggplant Caponata

If you prefer caponata as an appetizer, try it cold on crackers or rye bread.

4 tablespoons oil, more if needed
1 medium eggplant, peeled, cut in 1-in. cubes
1/2 cup chopped celery
1/2 cup chopped onion
1 clove garlic, peeled, minced

1 (8-oz.) can tomato sauce
1 tablespoon sugar
2 tablespoons white-wine vinegar
6 large pimiento-stuffed olives, sliced
Salt to taste
Coarse-ground black pepper to taste

Heat oil in wok. Add eggplant, celery, onion and garlic. Stir-fry until celery and onion are tender. Add remaining ingredients. Season to taste with salt and pepper. Cover and steam for 10 to 15 minutes, stirring frequently. Serve hot as a vegetable accompaniment or cold as an appetizer. As a vegetable, makes 6 servings. As an appetizer, makes 8 to 10 servings.

White Beans With Tomato & Garlic

Make ahead to have on hand for a quick supper.

1-1/2 cups dried navy beans or other white beans
Water
2 tablespoons oil
1 clove garlic, peeled and finely chopped
2 large tomatoes, coarsely chopped
1/4 cup water
1 teaspoon dried basil
1/2 teaspoon salt
1/4 teaspoon coarse-ground black pepper
1 tablespoon vinegar
2 tablespoons minced parsley

Put beans in a colander and rinse under cold water. Place in a large pot and cover with water. Bring to a full boil over high heat and let boil briskly about 2 minutes. Remove from heat and let the beans soak in the warm water, uncovered, about 1 hour. Reheat and bring to a full boil. Lower heat and simmer for 1 to 1-1/2 hours or until the beans are tender. Add additional water if necessary to keep beans covered with water while cooking. Drain. Heat oil in wok over moderate heat. Add garlic and stir-fry about 30 seconds. Add tomatoes and stir-fry about 1 minute. Pour in 1/4 cup water. Cover and steam for 1 minute. Uncover and chop tomato. Add beans, basil, salt, pepper and vinegar. Cook, stirring often until beans are reheated, about 10 minutes. Add additional salt if needed. Sprinkle with parsley just before serving. Makes 6 to 8 servings.

EGGS

There's no limit to what you can do with the versatile egg. Great-tasting main courses, Sunday morning ham and eggs, eggs with a Chinese accent, an Italian touch or a Spanish flair. All easy, inexpensive and wonderfully good for you. Few foods can match eggs as a top-quality source of low-calorie protein.

But why wok-cooked eggs? Eggs are fragile and if overcooked they become rubbery and tasteless. The intense heat of a wok lets you cook your egg dishes fast without danger of overcooking. Whether stir-fried or steamed, wok-cooked eggs keep their delicate flavor.

Someone once said the most perfect package in the world is a banana. I think it's an egg. An egg holds its contents to perfection and one thing is sure, if it breaks and becomes contaminated you *know* it.

I hope you will enjoy the egg dishes. I find them to be the answer when searching for something delicious, easy and inexpensive.

SUNDAY MORNING DELUXE

Orange Juice & Champagne (half & half)
Breakfast Ham & Eggs, page 80
Miniature Danish
Coffee

Brussels Sprouts With Anchovies, page 48
Cheese Timbales With Vegetables, page 84
Rum Cake, page 249

Scrambled Eggs Italian-Style

Perfect for a tasty economical supper.

2 tablespoons bacon fat
1/2 cup chopped onion
1/4 cup chopped green pepper
1 clove of garlic, peeled, minced
1 (1-lb.) can tomatoes, drained; reserve juice
2 teaspoons cornstarch dissolved in 1/4 cup juice from
 tomatoes
3 to 4 drops red-hot-pepper sauce
1/4 teaspoon mixed Italian herbs
1/2 teaspoon salt
1/4 teaspoon pepper
6 slices cooked bacon, drained and crumbled
1 tablespoon bacon fat
5 large eggs
Salt to taste
1/4 cup minced parsley
Thick-sliced Italian bread

Heat wok. Add 2 tablespoons bacon fat; melt over medium heat. Add onion, pepper and garlic. Stir-fry about 5 to 6 minutes until vegetables are limp. Add tomatoes, dissolved cornstarch, pepper sauce, Italian herbs, salt and pepper. Cook, stirring, about 6 to 8 minutes or until sauce thickens. Place on a platter or shallow baking dish. Arrange crumbled bacon around edge of platter. Wipe wok clean with paper towel. Add 1 tablespoon bacon fat and place over medium heat. When melted and hot, add eggs and stir-fry until set. Spoon over center of sauce. Sprinkle with salt and minced parsley. Serve with thick slices of Italian bread. Makes 4 servings.

Breakfast Ham & Eggs

Would you believe ham and eggs in a wok?

1 tablespoon heavy cream, room temperature
1 slice ham, room temperature, trimmed to fit small
   ramekin or small baking dish
2 eggs, room temperature
1 tablespoon heavy cream, room temperature
Salt and pepper to taste
Butter slivers

Place 1 tablespoon of cream in a ramekin or similar small baking dish such as a custard cup. Cover with a slice of ham. Break two eggs over the ham. Spoon 1 tablespoon of cream over the eggs. Sprinkle with salt and pepper to taste. Dot with butter slivers. Place ramekin on rack in wok over simmering water. Cover and seal ramekin with foil. Cover wok and steam for 8 to 10 minutes or until egg whites are set but yolks are still soft. Makes 1 serving.

Eggs With Rice

A nifty egg stretcher.

1 tablespoon oil
1/2 teaspoon salt
1 cup long-grain rice
1 cup chicken broth
1 cup water
4 eggs
1/2 teaspoon soy or Worcestershire sauce
2 tablespoons melted butter
Salt and pepper to taste
Soy or Worcestershire sauce, if desired

Heat oil with salt in wok. Add rice and stir until grains are coated with oil. Pour in broth and water. Bring to a boil, stirring frequently. Cover wok. Lower heat and steam until rice is tender and almost all liquid has been absorbed. Remove wok from heat. Let stand, covered, until all liquid has been absorbed by rice. Beat eggs with soy or Worcestershire sauce. Return wok to low heat. Add butter and immediately stir in eggs. Stir until eggs are set. Remove wok from heat. Season with salt and pepper to taste. If desired, sprinkle each serving with soy or Worcestershire sauce. Makes 4 to 6 servings.

Cheese Timbales With Vegetables

Very colorful, truly delicious and low calorie.

1/4 lb. green beans, ends trimmed
1 tablespoon minced green onion
1 tablespoon lemon juice
1/3 teaspoon salt
2 eggs
1/2 cup milk
3 tablespoons grated sharp Cheddar cheese
Salt to taste
2 small zucchini, trimmed, sliced thin at 45-degree angle
1 small tomato, cut in half, seeded
2 tablespoons minced green onion
2 tablespoons lemon juice
1/3 teaspoon salt
1 teaspoon sugar
Paprika, for garnish

Lightly butter two 1/2-cup timbale molds or custard cups.
Place green beans on one side of a shallow 10-inch-round
baking dish. Sprinkle with 1 tablespoon green onion, 1
tablespoon lemon juice and 1/3 teaspoon salt. Place dish
on rack in wok over simmering water. Cover and steam for
15 minutes. While beans cook, beat eggs with milk until
blended. Add cheese and salt to taste. Pour into buttered
timbale molds or custard cups. Place on baking dish with
beans. Cover and steam for 15 minutes. Arrange zucchini
and tomato halves on the baking dish. Sprinkle with 2
tablespoons green onion, 2 tablespoons lemon juice and
1/3 teaspoon salt. Sprinkle sugar on tomato halves. Cover.
Steam vegetables and timbales for 15 minutes. Unmold
timbales or custard cups onto serving plates, sprinkle with
paprika and surround with vegetables. Makes 2 servings.

Blend eggs and milk together. Stir in cheese and salt.

Pour mixture into timbale molds and place on baking dish in wok with green beans. Steam for 15 minutes. Add zucchini and tomatoes to the baking dish and steam for another 15 minutes.

Timbales Petits Pois

Transform an ordinary vegetable into rich elegance.

2 tablespoons butter
2 tablespoons minced green onion
1 cup tiny green peas, uncooked
2 tablespoons water
1/2 cup heavy cream
3 eggs
1/2 teaspoon salt
1/4 teaspoon pepper
1/8 teaspoon nutmeg
Minced parsley, for garnish

Butter four 1/2-cup timbale molds or custard cups. Melt butter in a small saucepan. Add green onion, peas and water. Cover and steam until peas are tender. Pour into an electric blender. Blend at high speed until pureed. Add cream and eggs. Blend only until smooth. Season with salt, pepper and nutmeg. Pour mixture into buttered timbale molds or custard cups. Place on a 10-inch-round shallow baking dish. Place dish on rack in wok over simmering water. Cover loosely with foil. Cover wok and steam about 30 minutes or until set. When done, a knife inserted in the center will come out clean. Turn out onto serving plate and sprinkle with minced parsley. Makes 4 servings.

Deviled Ham & Eggs

Easy, but so different and delicious!

1 tablespoon butter, room temperature
1 (2-1/4-oz.) can deviled ham
1/2 teaspoon mustard
1/4 teaspoon Worcestershire sauce
2 to 3 drops Tabasco® sauce
4 slices white bread, toasted
4 eggs
Salt and pepper to taste
Paprika, for garnish

Butter 4 custard cups. Mix together butter, deviled ham, mustard, Worcestershire sauce, and Tabasco® sauce. Spread on toasted bread. Break eggs into buttered custard cups. Sprinkle with salt and pepper to taste. Place on steamer rack in wok over simmering water. Cover wok and steam eggs about 15 minutes until set. Unmold onto ham toast and sprinkle with paprika. Makes 4 servings.

Eggs With Shrimp Bombay-Style

A touch of India adds spice to your meal.

6 large eggs
1 tablespoon cold water
1 teaspoon curry powder
1 teaspoon salt
1/4 teaspoon pepper
1/4 cup minced green onion

3 tablespoons peanut or safflower oil
6 ozs. frozen raw shrimp, peeled, deveined, thawed
1 tablespoon peanut or safflower oil
1 tablespoon butter
Mango Chutney, page 209

In a bowl beat eggs with water, curry powder, salt and pepper until blended. Add onion. Heat wok. Add 2 tablespoons oil. When hot add shrimp and stir-fry over medium heat until firm and pink. Remove with a slotted spoon to a warm plate. Pour oil from wok and wipe dry with paper towel. Add 1 tablespoon oil and butter. Place wok over moderate heat. When butter melts and begins to sizzle, add egg mixture. Stir gently. Add shrimp. Continue stirring until eggs are set. Serve with Mango Chutney as an accompaniment. Makes 4 servings.

Egg & Vegetable Stir-Fry

For Sunday-night supper, add crusty rolls and for dessert—steamed apples.

1 tablespoon oil
1 small green pepper, seeded and chopped
  (about 1/2 cup)
1/2 cup chopped onion
1 small hot chili pepper, seeded, finely chopped,
  if desired
6 eggs
1/4 cup sour cream
1 medium tomato, peeled, cut in eighths, seeds removed
Salt and pepper to taste
3 tablespoons butter

Heat oil in wok. Add green pepper, onion and chili peppers, if desired. Stir-fry until soft. Remove and set aside until cooled. In a bowl beat eggs with sour cream. Add stir-fried vegetables, tomato and salt and pepper to taste. Heat butter in wok. Add egg mixture. Cook stirring over medium heat until scrambled. Makes 3 to 4 servings.

Eggs With Chicken Livers

A splendid Sunday brunch!

1 tablespoon oil
1/4 cup chopped green onion
2 tablespoons butter
1/2 lb. chicken livers, each cut in 4 pieces
1/4 cup Madeira wine
2 tablespoons butter
8 eggs
1/2 teaspoon salt
1/4 teaspoon pepper
1 tablespoon minced parsley

Heat oil in wok. Add green onion and stir-fry until limp. Add 2 tablespoons butter. When melted and sizzling, add chicken livers. Stir-fry about 3 minutes until firm and cooked through center. Add wine, cover and steam for 1 minute. Uncover and stir-fry until liquid evaporates. Add 2 tablespoons butter. Beat eggs with salt, pepper and parsley. Pour into wok. Stir-fry to a soft but firm scramble. Makes 4 servings.

POULTRY

If you want to appreciate chicken, try cooking it in a wok. Stir-fry it with vegetables—or steam it with a savory stuffing—then glaze or deep-fry it in batter. Chicken and cornish hens—duck, too—are easily overcooked, but with fast, thorough wok cookery you can be sure the results will be delectable and predictable.

Chicken is truly adaptable. It works with every possible cooking method and most types of seasoning. As the base of literally dozens of dishes, it combines with other foods for an endless repertoire of great tasting "cooked-all-at-once-in-your-wok, almost no work and one-pot-to-wash" meals.

Many recipes start with steamed chicken. Amazingly enough, even a scrawny chicken will plump up and become juicy when steamed. All fowl cooks to perfection in a very short time. This is the perfect method to use when your recipe calls for cooked chicken.

More elaborate recipes follow. Their roots are in some great dishes of the past, but they are equally easy to prepare. For a really smash-success dinner party try Cornish Game Hens California-Style, page 96, or twice-cooked Glazed Duck, page 102. Or, the next time you are "just too tired and there is no joy in cooking" put together the recipe for Chicken & Almonds With Broccoli Hollandaise, page 117. It tastes as though a talented chef had spent hours in your kitchen, but you can do it in only five minutes.

Honestly, once you begin to wok cook your chicken, you'll believe that your wok is worth ten times its price.

With the enormous quantity of fresh chicken available, there is usually no reason to use the frozen variety. Frozen ducks do not seem to lose flavor by their stay in the cold, but other fowl are decidedly more flavorful when purchased fresh. Because you use less meat in wok-style cookery, this may offset the slightly higher cost of fresh over frozen.

LUNCHEON PARTY FOR THE GIRLS

Tomato & Clam Juice Cocktail
Chicken Breasts Maryland, With
Asparagus & Mushrooms, page 106
Apricots Imperatrice, page 240

FROM THE PHILIPPINES

Chicken, Pork & Shrimp en Adobo, page 101
Rice
Fresh Pears or Apples
Camembert Cheese

BLACK-TIE DINNER FOR FOUR

Artichoke Hearts Vinaigrette, page 47
Cornish Game Hens California-Style,
page 96
Tiny Peas With Pearl Onions
Avocado & Grapefruit Salad
Orange-Lemon Pudding, page 247

Chicken & Mushrooms in Brandy Cream

There are times when it's best to forget calories.

1/4 cup flour
1 teaspoon salt
1/4 teaspoon pepper
1 whole chicken breast, skinned, boned, cut into bite-size
   pieces
4 tablespoons butter
6 to 8 large mushrooms, trimmed, sliced lengthwise
   through stems
1/4 cup brandy
1 cup heavy cream
2 tablespoons catsup
2 to 3 dashes Tabasco® sauce
1 teaspoon cornstarch dissolved in 1 tablespoon water
Salt and pepper to taste
1/4 cup minced parsley
Crisp toast or patty shells
Parsley, for garnish

Combine flour, 1 teaspoon salt and 1/4 teaspoon pepper.
Coat chicken in flour mixture. Rub flour evenly into each
piece. Shake off excess. Heat wok, add 2 tablespoons of
the butter. When sizzling, add chicken pieces and brown
lightly on both sides. Remove with slotted spoon. Add
remaining butter and mushrooms to wok. Stir-fry over
medium heat about 5 minutes. Remove mushrooms with
slotted spoon. Remove wok from heat. Add brandy,
cream, catsup, Tabasco® sauce, dissolved cornstarch and
blend. Stir over low heat until sauce thickens. Add salt,
pepper, chicken and mushrooms. Stir until reheated.
Serve on toast or in patty shells. Sprinkle with parsley.
Makes 2 to 3 servings.

Chicken Rolls Kiev

Serve this classic for a special dinner.

3 whole chicken breasts, skinned, boned, halved
Juice from 1/2 lemon
Salt
2 tablespoons butter
1/2 cup flour
1 egg, beaten with 1 tablespoon water
1 cup fine dry bread crumbs
Oil, for frying
Sour Cream, for garnish
Paprika, for garnish

Pound each half chicken breast very thin between 2 sheets of wax paper. Sprinkle with lemon juice and salt. Place a teaspoon of butter on each and roll each up tightly. Tuck in sides to encase butter completely. Roll in flour, then in egg beaten with water, then in bread crumbs. Press crumbs into meat so each roll is completely coated. Refrigerate until chilled. Pour oil into wok to a 3-inch depth. Heat to 375°F (191°C) or until a one-inch cube of bread dropped in the oil browns in about 60 seconds. With tongs, lower 2 or 3 chicken rolls into hot fat and fry about 4 minutes until deep golden brown. Drain on paper towel. Arrange on warm plates and spoon a little sour cream over each serving. Sprinkle with paprika and serve at once. Makes 6 chicken rolls.

Chicken Livers & Mushrooms With Spaghetti

Budget special with elegant taste and appearance.

2 tablespoons oil
1/2 teaspoon salt
1/2 lb. chicken livers, trimmed and quartered
1 tablespoon oil
1/4 lb. mushrooms, trimmed, sliced thin lengthwise
   through stems
1/2 cup finely chopped onion
1 clove garlic, peeled, minced
1 (1-lb.) can Italian-plum tomatoes, chopped
1 tablespoon tomato paste
1/2 teaspoon sugar
1 cup chicken broth
2 teaspoons cornstarch
3 tablespoons brandy or sherry
1 (1-lb.) pkg. thin spaghetti, cooked

Heat 2 tablespoons oil with salt in wok. Add chicken livers. Stir-fry over medium heat until lightly browned. Remove livers and set aside. Wipe wok clean with paper towel. Add 1 teaspoon oil. Stir-fry mushrooms, onion and garlic until soft. Add tomatoes, tomato paste, sugar and broth. Bring to a boil. Lower heat and simmer for 15 minutes. Stir occasionally. Add browned livers. Stir until heated. Dissolve cornstarch in brandy or sherry. Add to wok. Stir until sauce thickens. Serve over hot cooked spaghetti. Makes 6 servings.

Turkey Madras

Make this dish your specialty!

2 tablespoons butter
1 tablespoon oil
1 small tart apple, peeled, seeded, cored, *very finely* chopped
1 medium onion, peeled, *very finely* minced
1 tablespoon butter
2 to 3 tablespoons Madras curry powder, or to taste
2 tablespoons flour
2-1/2 cups heated chicken broth
Salt to taste
Coarse-ground black pepper to taste
2 cups cubed cooked turkey
2 cups cooked rice
1/2 cup finely minced green onion
1/2 cup chopped dry roasted peanuts
1/2 cup finely minced parsley
Mango Chutney, page 207

Heat 2 tablespoons butter and the oil in wok. Add apple and onion. Cook, stirring frequently, over very low heat until apple can be easily mashed with a wooden spoon. Add 1 tablespoon butter. When melted, stir in curry powder and flour. Add heated broth and blend. Stir until sauce thickens. Season with salt and pepper to taste. Add turkey and stir until heated. Serve over rice. Sprinkle each serving with minced green onion, chopped peanuts and minced parsley. Serve with Mango Chutney. Makes 4 to 6 servings.

Chicken Californian

A beautiful blend of chicken, peas and olives.

2 tablespoons oil
1/4 cup minced onion
1 (10-oz.) pkg. frozen peas, partially thawed
1/4 cup unsweetened pineapple juice
1-1/2 to 2 cups cooked chicken
2 cups cooked rice
1/2 cup coarsely chopped green olives
1/2 cup coarsely chopped black olives
1/4 cup capers, drained
Salt to taste

Heat oil in wok. Add onion and stir-fry until limp. Add peas and stir-fry about 30 seconds. Pour in pineapple juice and cover. Steam until peas are tender, stirring frequently. Add chicken. Stir about 30 seconds. Add remaining ingredients. Stir and toss gently until heated. Add salt to taste. Makes 6 servings.

Cornish Game Hens California-Style

A dish worthy of a five-star French restaurant.

2 Cornish game hens
1/2 cup oil
Juice from 2 large lemons
1/4 cup light-brown sugar, firmly packed
1 tablespoon Worcestershire sauce
2 tablespoons catsup

2 tablespoons minced green onion
1 clove garlic, peeled and finely minced
3/4 cup sherry
1/2 teaspoon salt
Walnut-Date Stuffing, see below
2 teaspoons cornstarch

Walnut-Date Stuffing:

1 tablespoon flour
1/4 cup shelled, broken walnuts
8 pitted dates
1 teaspoon minced onion
1 cup herb-seasoned stuffing mix
3/4 cup water

Rinse hens inside and out under cold running water. Blot dry with paper towel. Prick skin of each hen in several places with fork tines. Place in a deep baking dish. Combine remaining ingredients except stuffing and cornstarch and pour over hens. Cover and refrigerate 12 to 24 hours. Turn hens in marinade frequently. Drain; reserve marinade. Stuff each bird with Walnut-Date Stuffing. Place in a shallow baking dish on rack in wok over simmering water. Cover loosely with foil. Cover wok and steam for 1 hour. Remove from wok. Strain reserved marinade into a saucepan. Place over medium heat, simmer until reduced by about half. Stir in cornstarch and cook until thickened. Spoon over hens in baking dish. Again place dish in wok on rack over simmering water and cover loosely with foil. Cover wok and steam for 15 minutes. Baste occasionally. Makes 4 servings.

Walnut-Date Stuffing:

Mix flour with walnuts and dates. Chop fine and mix with minced onion, stuffing mix and water.

Aloha Chicken

You can put this exotic meal on the table in 10 minutes!

2 tablespoons oil
1/2 teaspoon salt
1/2 cup diagonally sliced celery
1 cup water
2 cups diced cooked chicken
1 cup quick-cooking long-grain rice
1 (10-oz.) pkg. frozen Hawaiian-style stir-fry vegetables
   with seasoning mix, partially thawed
2 tablespoons soy sauce

Heat oil and salt in wok. Add celery. Stir-fry about 1 minute. Stir in water. Bring to a boil. Add chicken and rice, return to boil and cover wok. Lower heat and simmer for 3 minutes. Stir in partially thawed vegetables, seasoning mix and soy sauce. Cover and steam for 3 to 5 minutes. Stir occasionally until vegetables are hot and crisp-tender. Makes 4 to 6 servings.

Cuban Chicken

Festive main dish for a buffet supper.

1/4 cup vegetable or peanut oil
1 clove garlic, peeled and minced
1 small purple onion, peeled, chopped
1/2 of 10-oz. pkg. frozen peas, thawed
1 (1-lb.) can whole peeled tomatoes, drained
   and chopped

3 cups cold cooked rice
1 cup slivered cooked ham
2 cups boned, skinned, bite-size cubes steamed chicken
1/2 cup sliced pimiento-stuffed olives
1 medium avocado, peeled, pitted, sliced lengthwise
Pimiento strips for garnish

Heat wok, add oil, garlic, onion and peas. Stir-fry about 2 to 3 minutes until onion is soft. Add tomatoes, rice, ham, chicken and olives. Stir and lift until heated. Place in center of a large platter. Surround with slices of avocado. Garnish with pimiento. Makes 4 to 6 servings.

Steamed Chicken

Easy and economical, steamed chicken plumps up and retains its flavor.

1 (4- to 5-lb.) roasting chicken
6 cloves garlic, peeled
1/2 lemon
1 apple, quartered
3 tablespoons very cold butter, cut in slivers and frozen
Salt
1/2 cup sherry

Wash and dry the chicken. Place garlic, lemon and apple inside cavity. Pull skin slightly away from chicken breast. With your fingers insert butter slivers under skin, pushing them up as far as possible. Rub chicken with salt. Place in shallow heat-proof dish. Pour sherry over chicken. Place dish on rack in wok over simmering water. Cover, steam for 1 hour or until chicken is very tender. Remove chicken and cool. Remove skin and bone. Cut meat in bite-size pieces. Place in storage dish. Cover tightly and refrigerate until ready to use. Makes about 3 cups cooked chicken.

Chicken Broth

Essential for full-bodied flavor in many chicken and pork dishes.

1 (2-1/2- to 3-lb.) stewing chicken
Water
1 large onion, peeled, quartered
3 carrots, peeled and cut in chunks
3 cloves garlic, split
3 or 4 celery stalks with leaves
Several sprigs parsley
1/2 cup dry white wine
1 teaspoon salt

Place the chicken in a 5-quart pot. Add water. Bring to a boil and skim off film that rises to top. Add onion, carrots, garlic, celery, parsley, wine and salt. Lower heat to a simmer and cook until chicken is tender, about 1 hour. Remove chicken from broth. Cool slightly, remove meat from bones; refrigerate until needed. Return bones and any scraps of meat or skin to broth and allow to cook over very low heat for about 2 hours. Strain broth into a large bowl. Discard bones and vegetables. Refrigerate broth until fat rises to surface and congeals. Remove and discard fat. Transfer broth to freezer containers and freeze until needed. Makes about 3 or 4 cups broth.

Chicken, Pork & Shrimp en Adobo

A wonderful mélange of flavors from the Philippines.

1 whole chicken breast, skinned, boned, cut in
   2-in. cubes
1/2 lb. fillet of pork, cut in 2-in. cubes
5 tablespoons cider vinegar
1 clove garlic, peeled, split and crushed
2 bay leaves
1 teaspoon salt
Chicken broth
3 tablespoons butter
1/2 lb. raw shrimp, peeled and deveined
2 or 3 tablespoons Madeira wine
Salt and pepper to taste
3 cups hot cooked rice

Place chicken and pork cubes in a non-metal bowl. Add
vinegar, garlic, bay leaves and salt. Let stand 10 minutes.
Transfer to wok. Pour in enough chicken broth to cover
meat. Cover and simmer until all liquid has evaporated.
Add butter. When melted add shrimp and wine. Stir-fry
until shrimp are firm and pink. Season to taste with salt
and pepper. Remove bay leaves. Serve over rice. Makes 6
servings.

Plum Sauce

Serve with anything from Indian curry to fried chicken.

1 (1-lb.) jar damson plum preserves
1 tablespoon cider vinegar
1/4 cup sherry
1 (1-in.) cube fresh ginger, peeled, finely minced
1 clove garlic, peeled
1 teaspoon salt
2 teaspoons chili powder
2 tablespoons (canned) green chili peppers

In a small saucepan, combine ingredients. Cook, stirring over low heat until jam melts. Remove and discard garlic. Pour sauce into jars. Refrigerate when cooled. Will keep several weeks. Makes 1-1/2 cups sauce.

Glazed Duck

Two hours makes world-renowned Peking Duck.

1 (3-1/2- to 4-lb.) duck, thawed
4 cloves garlic, peeled
1/2 lemon
1 small tart apple, peeled, seeded and quartered
4 tablespoons cornstarch
1 cup oil
1/2 teaspoon salt
1/2 cup brown sugar, firmly packed

1 tablespoon Worcestershire sauce
Juice of 1 lemon
2 to 3 drops Tabasco® sauce
2 medium-long sweet potatoes, peeled and cut in
   1/2-in. rounds
3 medium turnips, peeled, cubed

Rinse duck inside and out under cold running water. Cut off fatty flap at tail end. Place garlic, lemon and apple in cavity. With a fork pierce skin in several places. Place duck on rack in wok over simmering water. Cover and steam for 25 minutes per pound, or until meat is almost falling off wing bones. Remove from wok and cool slightly. Cut off wings and discard. Cut duck in half. Remove and discard back and breast bones. Cut crosswise into quarters and blot dry with paper towel. Pour cooking liquid from wok and dry wok with paper towel. Rub cornstarch into each piece of duck. Pour oil in wok, add salt. Place over high heat until oil is hot, 375°F (191°C). Brown duck in hot oil, 1 piece at a time. Drain on paper towel. Pour cooking oil from wok. In a small saucepan combine brown sugar, Worcestershire sauce, lemon juice and Tabasco® sauce. Stir over moderate heat until sugar dissolves. Spoon mixture over duck in a shallow pan and let stand for 15 minutes, basting often. Place sweet-potato rounds in a shallow baking dish. Place dish on rack in wok over simmering water. Cover and steam 15 minutes. Push potatoes to side of dish. Add turnips. Cover and steam 5 minutes. Push turnips to side of baking dish. Place duck in center of dish. Cover and steam for 10 minutes or until vegetables are tender and duck is reheated and well glazed. Makes 4 servings.

Charleston Chicken & Rice

*Down in South Carolina this is called
Pilau Charlestonian.*

1 tablespoon oil
1/4 cup minced green onions
1 cup long-grain rice
1 cup chicken broth
1 cup water
1-1/2 teaspoons paprika
1/4 teaspoon pepper
1/2 teaspoon salt
2 cups diced cooked chicken or turkey
1/4 cup sliced pimiento
1 tablespoon Sauce Diable or
   1 teaspoon Worcestershire sauce and
   1 teaspoon prepared mustard

Heat oil in wok. Add green onion and stir-fry until soft. Stir in rice until grains are coated with oil. Pour in broth and water. Add paprika, pepper and salt. Stir only until blended. Bring to a boil. Cover and reduce heat. Simmer until rice is tender and almost all liquid has been absorbed. Add chicken and pimiento. Stir gently to blend. Remove wok from heat and let stand, covered, for about 10 minutes. Stir in Sauce Diable or Worcestershire sauce with mustard. If necessary, return wok to low heat. Toss and stir gently with a fork until reheated. Makes 6 servings.

Asopao

A delicious medley of flavors in a one-dish Puerto-Rican meal.

4 chicken thighs
4 chicken legs
1/2 teaspoon salt
1/2 teaspoon mixed Italian herbs
1/4 teaspoon pepper
1/4 cup oil
1 clove garlic, peeled, crushed
1/4 cup oil
1/2 cup chopped onions
1/4 cup chopped green peppers
1/2 cup slivered cooked ham
2 cups chicken broth
1 (1-lb.) can stewed tomatoes
1 cup converted long-grain rice
1 cup cooked green peas or frozen peas, thawed
4 oz. cleaned, deveined, frozen raw shrimp, thawed
6 to 8 pimiento-stuffed green olives, sliced
French bread

In a medium bowl place chicken thighs and legs. Sprinkle with salt, herbs and pepper. Pour 1/4 cup oil over chicken. Turn in oil until evenly coated. Add garlic. Let stand at room temperature for 1 hour. Heat remaining oil in wok. Over medium heat, brown 2 or 3 chicken pieces at a time. Remove as browned and set aside. Add onion, green pepper and ham. Stir-fry about 1 minute. Pour in broth and tomatoes. Stir to blend. Bring to a boil. Lower heat, return chicken pieces to wok and cover. Simmer about 30 minutes or until chicken is tender. Remove chicken from wok. Add rice to simmering sauce. Cook uncovered 5 minutes, stirring frequently. Cover and cook about 20 minutes or until rice is tender. Uncover and stir occasionally. Add peas, shrimp, olives and cooked chicken. Stir into rice and sauce. Cover. Simmer for 5 minutes or until shrimp are firm and pink and mixture is bubbly hot. All liquid will not be absorbed by rice. Serve Asopao in deep soup bowl with crusty French bread to mop up the sauce. Makes 4 to 6 servings.

Chicken Breasts Maryland

Asparagus and mushrooms make this luxurious entree.

2 chicken breasts, boned, skinned, halved
1 teaspoon minced onion
1 tablespoon lemon juice
1/2 teaspoon salt
4 thin slices baked ham
16 fresh asparagus spears
8 large mushroom caps
Paprika, for garnish
Sauce Supreme, see below

Sauce Supreme:

2 tablespoons butter
2 tablespoons flour
1 cup fat-free chicken broth
1/4 cup sherry
1 egg yolk
Salt and pepper to taste

Flatten each chicken breast with a mallet or side of heavy cleaver. Place in a shallow baking dish. Sprinkle with minced onion, lemon juice and salt. Place on rack in wok over simmering water and cover. Steam about 20 to 25 minutes or until breasts are tender. Remove from baking dish. Cover loosely with foil and set aside in a warm place. Remove and discard onion and cooking liquid from dish, wipe clean with paper towel. Cut ham slices into ovals a little larger than chicken breasts. Place asparagus and mushrooms in baking dish. Cover with ham slices. Place on rack in wok over simmering water. Steam for 15 minutes or until vegetables are tender. Prepare Sauce Supreme while ham and vegetables steam. Place steamed ham slices on serving plates. Cover each with a chicken breast. Arrange two asparagus and one mushroom on each side of chicken on each plate. Cover with Sauce Supreme and sprinkle with paprika. Makes 4 servings.

Sauce Supreme:

In a saucepan melt butter over low heat. Stir in flour. When bubbly, slowly add broth, stirring constantly. Cook, stirring until sauce is thick and smooth. Add sherry and beaten egg yolk. Beat until blended. Season to taste with salt and pepper. Cook a final minute, stirring.

Turkey & Rice Basque-Style

Spicy sausage, garlic and Italian herbs make this a snappy dish.

1 lb. hot Italian sausage
Water
2 tablespoons oil
2 medium green peppers, seeded, cut in julienne strips
1 small onion, peeled, chopped
1 clove garlic, peeled and finely minced
1 (1-lb.) can tomatoes with basil
1 teaspoon mixed Italian herbs
Salt to taste
Coarse-ground black pepper to taste
1 tablespoon tomato paste
3 cups cold cooked rice
4 to 5 large slices cold roast-turkey meat, cut in bite-size
    pieces

In a small skillet, cover sausage with water and bring to a boil. Prick sausage in several places with a knife. Simmer for 10 minutes. Drain and slice 1/2-inch thick. Heat oil in wok. Add green peppers, onion and garlic. Stir-fry until limp. Add sausage and stir-fry about 2 to 3 minutes. Add tomatoes, Italian herbs, salt, pepper and tomato paste. Stir-fry over high heat about 2 or 3 minutes. Add rice and turkey. Stir and lift until well mixed and heated. Makes 6 servings.

Apricot-Curry Glazed Chicken

Easy and elegant with a spicy sweet glaze.

8 chicken thighs
1/4 cup sherry
1/2 teaspoon garlic salt
4 teaspoons cornstarch
1 cup oil
1/2 teaspoon salt
1/2 cup apricot jam
1 teaspoon curry powder

With a fork pierce each chicken thigh in several places through skin side. Place skin-side up in a single layer in a shallow baking dish. Sprinkle with sherry and garlic salt. Turn skin-side down and let stand about 30 minutes. Pour off sherry and reserve. Turn chicken skin-side up in baking dish. Place dish on rack in wok over simmering water. Cover and steam about 25 minutes. Remove chicken pieces from wok and wipe thoroughly dry with paper towels. Rub cornstarch into each piece. Pour water from wok and wipe dry. Add oil and salt. Heat to almost sizzling. Fry chicken one thigh at a time in the hot oil until lightly browned. Pour oil from wok. In a small bowl, combine apricot jam, curry powder and 2 tablespoons of the reserved sherry. Blend well. Place chicken in a shallow baking dish and spoon jam mixture over. Let stand about 15 minutes. Baste frequently with jam mixture. Place dish in wok over simmering water. Cover and steam for 10 minutes or until chicken is reheated and well glazed. Makes 4 servings.

Chicken in Sherry Cream Sauce

Mushrooms, peas and tiny white onions complete this quick one-dish meal.

1 (10-oz.) pouch frozen green peas with tiny white onions
2 tablespoons oil
4 to 6 large fresh mushrooms, trimmed, sliced thin
   lengthwise through stems
1 whole chicken breast, skinned, boned and cut in
   bite-size pieces
2 tablespoons chicken broth
2 tablespoons dry sherry
Salt and pepper to taste

Remove green peas and onions from pouch and partially thaw. Heat oil in wok. Add mushrooms. Stir-fry over medium heat about 3 minutes. Add chicken pieces. Continue stir-frying until chicken is white and firm. Add partially thawed peas, onions, broth and sherry. Cook over low heat. Stir and break up block of vegetables as they cook. When vegetables are thawed, uncover, and stir-fry until sauce is hot and thick. Season to taste with salt and pepper. Makes 4 servings.

Chicken Salad Almondine

Gorgeous chicken salad—fit for a king.

2 cups cold steamed chicken, cut in bite-size pieces,
   see page 97
2 cups diced celery
2 cups seedless green grapes, halved
1 cup slivered almonds
1 cup Never-Fail Curry Mayonnaise, see below
Crisp Boston lettuce leaves
Fresh pineapple chunks, if desired

Never-Fail Curry Mayonnaise:

2 egg yolks
2 tablespoons lemon juice
1 teaspoon sugar
1/4 teaspoon salt
1 cup salad oil, not olive oil
2 teaspoons curry powder

Combine chicken, celery, grapes and almonds with Never-Fail Curry Mayonnaise. Chill 3 hours or more, to allow flavors to mellow. Spoon onto lettuce leaves on chilled plates. Garnish with pineapple chunks. Serve cold. Makes 4 to 6 servings.

Never-Fail Curry Mayonnaise

Combine egg yolks, lemon juice, sugar, and salt in electric blender. Blend one minute. With blender on high speed, add oil, a little at a time. Add curry powder and blend 1 minute longer.

Stir-Fry Chicken With Peaches

Surprise combination for an elegant party.

1 (2-1/2- to 3-lb.) chicken, cut in 8 pieces
1 teaspoon salt
1/2 teaspoon poultry seasoning
3 tablespoons cornstarch
1 cup oil
1 tablespoon oil
1 clove garlic, peeled, crushed
8 oz. frozen unsweetened peaches, thawed
1 tablespoon sugar
2 tablespoons lemon juice
1/2 cup chicken broth
2 teaspoons cornstarch dissolved in 1 tablespoon water
1 (10-oz.) pkg. frozen snow peas
3 cups hot cooked rice

Place chicken in a shallow baking dish. Sprinkle with salt and poultry seasoning. Place dish on rack in wok over simmering water. Cover, steam chicken for 45 minutes. Remove from wok and blot chicken dry with paper towels. Rub cornstarch into each piece. Pour water from wok and wipe dry. Add 1 cup oil and heat almost to sizzling. Fry chicken pieces in oil, 2 or 3 at a time until lightly browned. Remove as browned and set aside. Pour oil from wok. Add 1 tablespoon of oil to wok. Add garlic and stir-fry until browned. Remove and discard garlic. Add thawed peaches and sugar. Stir until heated. Stir in lemon juice. Add broth, heat to boiling. Stir in dissolved cornstarch. Add snow peas, stirring them into the liquid. Cover, steam for 30 seconds. Return browned chicken to wok. Cover and steam for 30 seconds or until chicken is reheated. Serve over hot cooked rice. Makes 6 to 8 servings.

How to Make Stir-Fry Chicken With Peaches

Place seasoned chicken in a baking dish on rack in the wok over simmering water. Steam 45 minutes.

Fry cornstarch-coated chicken in oil until lightly browned. Set aside.

Add chicken to peaches and sauce in the wok. Steam to reheat for 30 seconds. Serve over hot cooked rice.

Chicken & Cashews

Robust cabbage with a cashew nut surprise.

1 lb. boneless chicken breasts, cut in thin strips
2 tablespoons soy sauce
1 tablespoon cornstarch
2 tablespoons oil
1/2 teaspoon salt
1 small onion, peeled, chopped
1/2 lb. mushrooms, trimmed, sliced thin lengthwise
   through stems
2 tablespoons oil
1 small cabbage, shredded (about 4 cups)
1 teaspoon sugar
1 (6-oz.) pkg. cashew nuts, salt rinsed off, patted dry
1 teaspoon cornstarch
1/4 cup soy sauce
1 (3-oz.) can Chinese fried noodles

In a small bowl, place chicken strips with 2 tablespoons soy sauce and 1 tablespoon cornstarch. Blend well. Let stand at room temperature for 15 minutes. Heat 2 tablespoons oil with 1/2 teaspoon salt in wok over high heat. Add chicken strips and stir-fry until white and firm. Add onion and mushrooms. Continue to stir-fry until vegetables are soft. Place in a heated bowl. Add remaining 2 tablespoons of oil to wok. Stir in cabbage and sugar. Stir-fry about 3 to 4 minutes until cabbage is crisp-tender. Return chicken-vegetable mixture to wok. Add cashews, toss to combine with cabbage. Add 1 teaspoon cornstarch to 1/4 cup soy sauce. Stir into chicken-cashew mixture. Cover and steam for 1 minute. Uncover and stir until sauce is thickened. Sprinkle with Chinese fried noodles just before serving. Makes 4 to 6 servings.

Curried Chicken With Peas

Hawaii inspired this spicy recipe for leftover chicken.

2 tablespoons oil
1/2 teaspoon salt
1 small white onion, peeled, chopped
1 to 2 tablespoons curry powder
1-1/2 cups chicken broth
1 (10-oz.) pkg. frozen peas, partially thawed
2 teaspoons cornstarch dissolved in 1/4 cup
    unsweetened pineapple juice
1-1/2 cups diced cooked chicken
2 cups hot cooked rice

Heat oil with salt in wok. Add onion. Stir-fry about 30 seconds. Stir in curry powder. Slowly pour in broth, stirring as added. Bring to a boil. Add peas and cover. Simmer for 2 minutes. Stir dissolved cornstarch into simmering broth until sauce thickens. Add diced chicken. Cook, stirring until heated. Serve over hot cooked rice. Makes 4 servings.

Chicken Tamales

Easy, delicious and unusual.

1/4 lb. slab bacon, rind removed, cut in small cubes
1 green pepper, coarsely chopped
1 clove garlic, peeled
2 teaspoons chili powder
1/2 cup chicken broth
1 (12-oz.) can cream-style corn

1/2 cup jalapeño chili relish
1 teaspoon salt
1 teaspoon ground cumin
1 teaspoon fresh-ground black pepper
1-1/2 cups yellow cornmeal
1-1/2 cups finely shredded chicken
Butter
1 (8-oz.) can enchilada sauce, if desired

Stir-fry bacon in wok until crisp. Remove with a slotted spoon and reserve. Add green pepper, garlic and chili powder to fat in wok. Stir-fry until vegetables are limp. Combine in blender with bacon cubes, broth, corn, jalapeño relish, salt, cumin and pepper. Blend at high speed until smooth. Pour into a large mixing bowl. Add cornmeal and blend until you have a stiff paste. Add additional cornmeal if necessary. Generously butter 24 (7-1/4-inch) lengths of aluminum foil. Spoon about 1 tablespoon of the corn mixture in an oblong shape on each piece of foil. Place about 1-1/2 teaspoons shredded chicken in the center. Cover with an additional 1-1/2 tablespoons of corn mixture; smooth edges with your fingers. Fold foil over the tamale; double-fold the edge to make a seal. Fold foil ends the same way, leaving space to allow for slight expansion. Place on rack in wok over simmering water. Cover and steam for 1-1/2 hours. Add additional water to wok if necessary. Remove from foil and serve hot with enchilada sauce if desired. Makes 24 tamales.

Variation:

Substitute shredded cooked pork for chicken.

Tamales freeze well. Leave in foil packets and freeze until needed. To reheat, steam in wok for 30 minutes.

Chicken & Almonds With Broccoli Hollandaise

An eye and palate pleaser for a festive luncheon.

2 chicken breasts, skinned, boned
1 tablespoon minced onion
1 tablespoon minced fresh ginger root or 1/4 teaspoon
  ground ginger
1/4 cup sherry
1 tablespoon lemon juice
1 (10-oz.) pouch frozen broccoli in cheese sauce
1/4 cup grated mild Cheddar cheese
1/4 cup slivered almonds

Cut chicken breasts in large bite-size pieces. Place in a long shallow baking dish. Sprinkle with onion, ginger, sherry and lemon juice. Place on rack in wok over simmering water. Place cooking pouch of frozen broccoli and cheese sauce on same rack. Cover and steam for 30 minutes or until chicken is tender. Cooking pouch will be hot and pliable. Remove pouch. Split open and pour broccoli and cheese sauce over chicken in baking dish. Add cheese and almonds. Stir to blend. Cover and steam until cheese is melted. Makes 4 servings.

Chicken With Summer Fruit

Melon and grapes make this a festive party dish.

1 (2-1/2- to 3-lb.) chicken, cut in 8 pieces, backbone
   removed and discarded
1/4 cup sherry
1 (1-in.) cube fresh ginger root, minced, or 1/4 teaspoon
   ground ginger
Salt to taste
Butter
2-1/2 cups water
1 (8-oz.) pkg. Armenian-wheat-pilaf mix
2 tablespoons oil
1 tablespoon curry powder
1/2 teaspoon salt
1 cup clear, fat-free chicken broth
1 cup fresh honeydew melon balls or cubes
1 cup fresh cantaloupe balls or cubes
1 cup seedless white grapes
1/2 cup chopped water chestnuts
1 tablespoon cornstarch dissolved in 1 tablespoon
   lemon juice and 2 tablespoons water

Place chicken pieces in a single layer in a long shallow baking dish. Add sherry, sprinkle with ginger and salt. Place on rack in wok over simmering water and cover. Steam for 1 hour or until meat can be pulled easily from bone. Pour cooking liquid into a measuring cup. Refrigerate until cold. Remove skin and bones from chicken. Cut meat in bite-size pieces. Cover and refrigerate. Pour off and measure fat from chilled cooking liquid, discard remaining liquid. Add sufficient butter to make a total of 4 tablespoons of fat. Place in a saucepan with water. Bring to a boil. Add pilaf mix and lower heat.

Cover and simmer for 15 minutes or until liquid has evaporated. Set aside, covered, at room temperature until ready to reheat. Before serving, place pilaf mix over low heat. Heat oil in wok. Add curry powder and salt and stir-fry about 30 seconds. Pour in broth and bring to full boil while stirring. Add chicken pieces, melon balls or cubes, grapes and water chestnuts. Cook, stirring, until heated. Stir in dissolved cornstarch and continue to cook, stirring until sauce thickens. Serve over heated pilaf. Makes 4 to 6 servings.

FISH & SEAFOOD

Fish and shellfish respond almost instantaneously to heat, so cooking them properly, not overcooking, is best done in a wok. To serve a successful fish dinner, never cook fish in water. Instead, steam it with flavorful seasonings or stir-fry it, so that no flavor is lost. You can deep-fry fish, but only until crisp and golden on the outside. However it's cooked, serve fish with a suitable sauce—one that will point up its distinctive taste and enhance its goodness.

Many would-be gourmets will tell you that one variety of fish is better than another for cooking a particular way. The truth is that the best fish to cook by any method is the freshest fish you can obtain. You can catch it yourself, sweet talk it from a fisherman friend or go early in the morning to the best fish market in town and ask for the catch of the day. First check to make sure you are getting what you have asked for: The eyes of the fish should be bright, clear and bulging. The gills should be reddish or pink and fresh-smelling and the scales should be bright, tight to the skin and shiny. The flesh should be firm and spring back when pressed. And, of course, no strong or unpleasant odor should be obvious.

How much to buy? My family likes fish and, because it's lighter fare than steak, I buy generously. As a general rule, buy one pound of whole fish for each person. Fish spoils easily; if you're not going directly home, or it's a hot day, have it packed in enough ice to last until you can put it in your own refrigerator.

But don't bypass fish if fresh isn't available. Frozen-food companies do a great job fast-freezing fish with little or no loss of flavor and texture. Keep frozen fish packaged in its original container in your freezer until you intend to use it. Thawed fish must be cooked at once. Frozen fillets, steaks and dressed fish may be steamed in a wok without thawing but you must, of course, allow additional time for the cooking process. Deep-fried or stir-fried fish or shellfish should be thawed before cooking. To thaw frozen fish or shellfish remove from the package, place in a colander and rinse with cold water. Blot dry and refrigerate. As soon as it's thawed, but still cold, it's time to start cooking. As with all wok cookery, the recipes here are fast to the table, extra easy and especially delicious. Even if you're not a true fish fan, you'll enjoy them.

STATE-OF-MAINE SUPPER
Fish Hash Deluxe, page 122
Coleslaw
Down-East Indian Pudding, page 234

ELEGANT, EASY AND DIFFERENT
Cocktail Won Ton, page 38
Plum Sauce, page 102
Flounder With Grapefruit, page 139
Steamed New Potatoes
Orange-Pineapple Bundt Cake, page 241

SATURDAY SPECIAL LUNCHEON

Artichoke Hearts Vinaigrette, page 47
Egg Foo Yong With Crab Meat, page 126
Mocha Velvet Cake, page 264

FOURTH-OF-JULY PORCH SUPPER

Salmon Steaks With Anchovy-Lemon Butter,
page 136
Steamed Fresh Corn on the Cob
Steamed New Potatoes
Old-Fashioned Deep-Fried Apple Pies,
page 256

Fish Hash Deluxe

Try this tasty fish dish on a cool winter night.

3 slices thick-sliced bacon, chopped
1 small onion, peeled, minced
1/2 cup chopped celery
2 cups diced cooked potatoes
1 cup cooked green peas
1/2 cup chopped pimiento, drained
2 cups cooked flaked fish, haddock, cod or tuna
Salt and pepper to taste
Tomato catsup, for garnish

Place bacon in wok over low heat. Cook until crisp and all fat rendered. Remove bacon. Drain on paper towel, crumble and set aside. Remove all but 2 tablespoons rendered bacon fat and set aside. Increase heat to medium high. Add onion and chopped celery. Stir-fry until soft. Add diced potatoes. If necessary, add a little more of the rendered bacon fat. Cook, stirring until lightly browned. Add peas, pimientos, fish and reserved bacon. Stir-fry only until heated. Season with salt and pepper to taste. Turn onto serving plate. If desired, garnish with catsup. Makes 4 servings.

Hawaiian Fish Fry

Make fish special with this pungent sauce.

1-1/2 lbs. fish fillets, cut crosswise in 2-in. strips
1 cup flour, mixed with 1 teaspoon salt, 1/2 teaspoon
   pepper
Oil for deep-frying
Hawaiian Sauce, see below

Hawaiian Sauce:

1/3 cup soy sauce
1 tablespoon lemon juice
1 tablespoon cider vinegar
2 tablespoons sugar
2 tablespoons catsup
1 tablespoon grated onion
Salt and pepper to taste

Blot fish strips dry. Rub flour mixture into each strip. Pour oil in wok to a 3-inch center depth. Heat to 375°F (191°C). Fry a few fish strips at a time in the hot oil until lightly browned. Pour Hawaiian Sauce over fried fish strips and serve. Makes 4 to 6 servings.

Hawaiian Sauce:

Combine sauce ingredients in small saucepan. Cook, stirring until well heated.

Scallops Provençale

A lovely low-calorie luncheon or supper dish.

1-1/2 lbs. scallops
1/2 cup flour
2 tablespoons oil
4 tablespoons butter
1 clove garlic, peeled and finely minced
2 tablespoons strained fresh lemon juice
1/2 cup finely minced parsley
Salt and pepper to taste
4 slices crisp toast

Wash and dry the scallops. Roll them in flour. Heat oil with butter and garlic in wok over medium heat. Add scallops. Stir-fry until firm, white and flecked with brown. Add lemon juice and parsley; season with salt and pepper to taste. Stir to blend and serve at once over crisp toast. Makes 4 servings.

Mackerel With Broccoli in Cheese Sauce

An unbeatable trio!

8 small new potatoes
1 (2-lb.) mackerel, cleaned
2 tablespoons oil
2 tablespoons sherry
1/4 cup chopped celery
1/4 cup chopped green onion
1 clove garlic, peeled, minced
1 teaspoon Worcestershire sauce
1 (10-oz.) pouch frozen broccoli in cheese sauce
2 teaspoons cornstarch dissolved in 2 tablespoons water

Place potatoes on rack in wok over simmering water. Cover wok and steam for 15 minutes. Make diagonal slits on each side of the fish, slashing it to the bone. Pour oil and sherry into a long shallow baking dish. Sprinkle with celery, onion, garlic and Worcestershire sauce. Place fish over vegetables. Place dish on rack with potatoes in wok over simmering water. Place pouch of partially thawed broccoli in sauce on same rack. Cover wok. Steam for 20 minutes or until fish flakes easily when touched with a fork and pouch of broccoli and sauce is extremely hot to the touch. Transfer fish to a heated platter. Open pouch of broccoli and sauce; pour into baking dish. Mix with celery, onion and garlic. Mix in dissolved cornstarch, stirring until thick and smooth. Pour over fish. Serve with new potatoes. Makes 4 servings.

Kedgeree

English Kedgeree is a nice change of pace and especially good on a cold winter evening.

1 (1-lb.) can salmon, reserve juice
4 hard-cooked eggs
2 cups cooked rice
1/4 cup minced parsley
1 tablespoon curry powder, or to taste
1-1/2 cups sour cream

Butter a 1-1/2 quart baking dish. Flake salmon; reserve juice. Slice the eggs. Place alternate layers of rice, salmon, sliced eggs and parsley in the buttered baking dish. Stir curry powder into sour cream and pour over mixture. Place in wok on rack over simmering water. Cover wok. Steam for 15 minutes or until thoroughly heated. Makes 6 servings.

Egg Foo Yong With Crab Meat

A little crab meat goes a long way.

1 tablespoon oil
1/2 cup trimmed and diced fresh mushrooms
3 large eggs
1/2 lb. crab meat, drained, cartilage removed, flaked
1/2 cup bean sprouts
2 tablespoons oil
Foo Yong Sauce, see below

Foo Yong Sauce:

1 cup chicken broth
1 tablespoon soy sauce
1/2 teaspoon sugar
1 tablespoon cornstarch dissolved in 2 tablespoons
  water
1/2 cup cooked green peas

Heat 1 tablespoon of the oil in wok. Add the mushrooms and stir-fry about 1 minute. Place in a bowl until cooled. Break the eggs in a second bowl. Beat well. Add stir-fried mushrooms, crab and bean sprouts. Add 1 teaspoon of the oil to the wok. Heat for 30 seconds over moderate heat. Pour in about 1/4 cup of the egg mixture. Cook without stirring for 1 minute or until very lightly browned on underside. Turn; cook until other side is also lightly browned. Transfer to a serving platter and cover loosely with foil to keep warm. Cook remaining egg mixture in the same way. Add about 1 teaspoon of oil to wok for each new omelet. Spoon Foo Yong Sauce over each omelet just before serving. Makes 6 small omelets.

Foo Yong Sauce:

Combine broth, soy sauce, sugar and dissolved cornstarch in a small saucepan. Stir over low heat until the sauce has thickened. Keep warm over low heat. Stir in peas just before serving.

Sweet & Sour Shrimp

An unusual & delicious way to serve shrimp.

1 carrot, peeled, diagonally sliced
Water
1 green pepper, cut in 1-in. squares
2 cups oil, for frying
1/2 teaspoon salt
1 (8-oz.) pkg. frozen breaded shrimp
1 tablespoon oil
1 clove garlic, peeled, flattened
Sweet & Sour Sauce, see below
1 cup unsweetened pineapple chunks, drain; reserve
   juice for sauce
3/4 cup mixed sweet pickles, drained
2 cups hot cooked rice

Sweet & Sour Sauce:

1 cup unsweetened pineapple juice
1/4 cup white wine vinegar
1 tablespoon soy sauce
1/3 cup brown sugar
1/4 cup catsup
2 tablespoons cornstarch
1/4 cup unsweetened pineapple juice

Place carrot slices in a saucepan and cover with water. Boil for 5 minutes. Add green pepper and continue to boil for 5 minutes. Drain and set aside. Pour 2 cups oil into wok. Add salt and heat to 375°F (191°C) or until a 1-inch cube of bread will brown in 50 to 60 seconds. Fry the frozen breaded shrimp, a few at a time, until lightly browned. Drain on paper towel and keep warm. Pour oil from wok. Wipe wok clean with paper towel. Add 1 tablespoon of oil.

Place over high heat. Add garlic and rub it against sides and bottom of wok until lightly browned. Remove and discard garlic. Add peppers and carrots. Stir-fry about 30 seconds. Pour in Sweet & Sour Sauce. Add pineapple chunks and pickles. Stir until very hot. Add fried shrimp and stir into sauce. Spoon over hot cooked rice and serve at once. Makes 4 servings.

Sweet & Sour Sauce:

In a small saucepan, combine 1 cup pineapple juice, vinegar, soy sauce, sugar and catsup. Stir over moderate heat to simmering. Dissolve cornstarch in 1/4 cup pineapple juice. Add to sauce. Set aside.

Tuna-Fish Curry

A unique way with low-cost tuna.

2 tablespoons oil
1 clove garlic, peeled, crushed
2 small tart apples, peeled, seeded and finely chopped
2 teaspoons curry powder, or to taste
1 (8-oz.) can tomato sauce
2 tablespoons sherry or dry white wine
1 (8-oz.) can tuna, drained and broken in chunks
2 cups hot cooked rice

Heat oil with garlic in wok. Cook, stirring until garlic is lightly browned. Remove and discard garlic. Add apple and stir-fry over medium heat about 1 to 2 minutes. Stir in curry powder. Add tomato sauce. Bring to a boil, add sherry or wine and tuna. Stir until heated. Serve over hot cooked rice. Makes 4 servings.

Fish With Deviled Sauce

Delicately steamed fish with a zippy sauce.

1 (1-1/2- to 2-lbs.) fresh white fish (flounder or sea bass)
2 tablespoons sherry
1 tablespoon oil
1 clove garlic, peeled
4 tablespoons Sauce Diable or
   1 teaspoon Worcestershire sauce and
   1 teaspoon prepared mustard
2 tablespoons lemon juice
1 teaspoon sugar
4 to 6 dashes Tabasco® sauce
1/2 cup finely slivered green onions
Thin slices of lemon, for garnish

Rinse the fish inside and out with cold water. Blot dry with a paper towel. Place in a heat-proof oval platter or in a shallow baking dish. Sprinkle with sherry. Put dish on rack in wok over simmering water. Cover wok and steam for 10 to 15 minutes depending on size of fish. When done, fish will flake easily if touched with a fork. While fish steams, heat oil in small saucepan and brown garlic over medium heat. Remove and discard garlic. Add Sauce Diable or Worcestershire sauce with mustard, lemon juice, sugar and Tabasco® sauce. Cook, stirring, until sauce begins to boil. To serve, pour sauce over steamed fish and sprinkle with green onions. Garnish with lemon slices. Makes 2 to 3 servings.

Swordfish Steaks With Cauliflower & Cheese Sauce

A gourmet meal—ready in 20 minutes!

2 swordfish steaks, about 1-in. thick
2 teaspoons oil
1/2 cup sherry or white wine
1/4 cup minced onion
1 (1-in.) cube finely minced fresh ginger root
1 (10-oz.) pouch frozen cauliflower with cheese sauce,
    partially thawed
1/4 cup thinly sliced pimiento-stuffed olives
2 teaspoons cornstarch dissolved in 2 tablespoons water

Place fish steaks in a long shallow baking dish. Spread with oil, pour in sherry or white wine. Sprinkle with onion and ginger. Place dish on rack in wok over simmering water. Place pouch of cauliflower and sauce on same rack. Cover wok and steam for 15 minutes. Remove cooking pouch, slit open and pour cauliflower and sauce over and around fish. Add olives, then gently stir in dissolved cornstarch to thicken sauce. Serve from the dish. Makes 4 servings.

Fritto Misto

An Italian-style deep-fry medley.

1 small eggplant, peeled, sliced, cut in 1- to
  1-1/2-in. strips
2 medium potatoes, peeled, sliced, cut in 1- to 1-1/2-in.
  strips
3 medium carrots, peeled, cut in 1- to 1-1/2-in. pieces
  and sliced in thin strips
Ice water
Juice of 1 large lemon
1-1/2 cups flour
1 teaspoon salt
1/2 teaspoon pepper
2 eggs, slightly beaten
1-1/2 cups fine dry bread crumbs
1/2 lb. firm white fish fillet cut crosswise into
  1-1/2-in. strips
Oil for deep frying

In a large bowl, place eggplant, potatoes and carrots.
Cover with ice water and stir in lemon juice. Let stand 1
hour. Drain, blot dry. Combine flour, salt and pepper.
Spread on wax paper. Coat vegetable strips in flour
mixture, dip in beaten egg and finally in bread crumbs.
Coat fish strips in the same way. When ready to fry, pour oil
in wok to a 3-inch center depth. Heat to 375°F (191°C). Fry
vegetables and fish in the hot oil, a few pieces at a time,
until they are golden brown. Drain on paper towel. Makes 6
servings.

Shrimp Chop Suey

Low-calorie shrimp and vegetables combine for a super-delicious supper.

2 tablespoons oil
1 small onion, peeled, chopped
1/4 lb. mushrooms, trimmed, sliced thin lengthwise
   through stems
1/2 lb. shrimp, cleaned, deveined, cut in half
1/2 cup water
1 (10-oz.) pkg. frozen Chinese-style stir-fry vegetables
   with seasoning mix, partially thawed
2 to 4 cups hot cooked rice

Heat oil in wok. Add onion and mushrooms. Stir-fry about 1 minute. Add shrimp. Stir-fry until firm and pink. Pour in water. Bring to a boil. Stir in Chinese vegetables; reserve package of seasoning mix. Return to a boil. Cover wok and lower heat. Steam for 2 to 3 minutes or until vegetables are heated through. Stir in vegetable-seasoning mix. Serve over hot cooked rice. Makes 4 to 6 servings.

Haddock Italian-Style

Serve this deliciously spiced fish with rice and green salad.

1 (12-oz.) pkg. frozen haddock fillets, partially thawed
Salt and pepper, to taste
1 large green pepper, seeded, cut in strips
1 medium onion, peeled, sliced, and separated into rings
2 teaspoons flour
1 (8-oz.) can Marinara sauce
1/4 teaspoon mixed Italian herbs

Cut block of fish crosswise into three equal parts. Place each piece on a 12-inch double thickness of foil. Sprinkle lightly with salt and pepper to taste. Top with pepper strips and onion rings. Stir flour into Marinara sauce until blended. Stir in Italian herbs and spoon over fish and vegetables. Bring foil edges together and fold them down, over and over 3 times. Fold each end over and over, making a loose package that is securely closed. The finished package should allow room at the top for steaming. Place in a shallow dish on rack in wok over simmering water. Cover and steam for 30 minutes or until fish flakes easily when touched with a fork. Makes 3 servings.

Trout With Pimiento Sauce

A beautiful, colorful way to serve small whole trout.

4 small trout, cleaned
1 tablespoon lemon juice
2 tablespoons sherry
Salt to taste
1 tablespoon oil
2 tablespoons butter
1/4 cup minced green onion
1 (4-oz.) jar chopped pimiento, drained
1 cup dry white wine
2 teaspoons cornstarch
1/4 cup chicken broth
Pitted black olives, for garnish
Lemon wedges, for garnish
Parsley sprigs, for garnish

Place trout on oval heat-proof platter or long shallow baking dish. Sprinkle both sides with lemon juice, sherry, salt and oil. Place on rack in wok over simmering water. Cover wok. Steam for 6 to 7 minutes or until fish flakes easily when touched with a fork. While fish steams, heat butter in a small saucepan over low heat. Add onion and sauté until limp. Stir in pimiento, add wine and bring to a boil. Reduce heat. Simmer until liquid is reduced by about half. Stir cornstarch into chicken broth. Stir into wine mixture until sauce thickens. Pour sauce over steamed fish. Garnish with olives, lemon and parsley. Serve from the cooking platter. Makes 4 servings.

Salmon Steaks With Anchovy-Lemon Butter

One of my favorite fish dishes.

2 (1-1/4-lb.) salmon steaks, 1 to 1-1/2-in. thick
1 (1-oz.) can flat anchovy fillets
1/4 lb. butter, room temperature
1/4 cup lemon juice
1/4 teaspoon coarse-ground black pepper
1/4 cup minced parsley
Lemon wedges, for garnish

Place salmon steaks on a heat-proof platter or in a shallow baking dish. Place on rack in wok over simmering water. Cover wok and steam for 15 to 20 minutes or until fish flakes easily when touched with a fork. While fish steams, mash anchovies to a paste in their own oil. Add to butter and cream until smooth. Beat in lemon juice and pepper. Spread some of the mixture over top of fish. Sprinkle with minced parsley. Garnish with lemon wedges. Serve remaining sauce separately. Makes 4 servings.

Variation:

Serve salmon steaks cold with Never-Fail Curry Mayonnaise, page 111, instead of Anchovy-Lemon Butter.

Shrimp in Hot Sauce

Spicy hot shrimp for a festive Friday night.

4 tablespoons butter, room temperature
36 large shrimp, cleaned, deveined
1 (8-oz.) can tomato sauce
4 or 5 drops red-hot-pepper sauce
1/4 cup lemon juice
1 teaspoon Worcestershire sauce
1 tablespoon bottled horseradish
Salt to taste
2 to 3 cups hot cooked rice or 4 to 6 pieces of toast

Heat wok. Add butter and melt over medium high heat. When butter begins to sizzle, add shrimp. Stir-fry about 5 minutes until shrimp are firm and pink. Add remaining ingredients and stir until bubbly hot. Serve over rice or with toast. Makes 4 to 6 servings.

New Orleans Jambalaya

A double-quick adaptation of a creole classic.

2 tablespoons oil
1/2 teaspoon salt
1/4 cup chopped green onion
1/4 cup chopped green pepper
6 oz. frozen, cleaned, deveined raw shrimp, partially
    thawed
1 (10-oz.) pkg. frozen New Orleans-style creole
    vegetables with seasoning mix, partially thawed,
    or mixed vegetables
1 cup boiling hot chicken broth
1-1/2 cups quick cooking long-grain rice
1 teaspoon cornstarch dissolved in 1 tablespoon water

Heat oil with salt in wok. Add onion and green pepper. Stir-fry over high heat about 30 seconds. Add frozen shrimp and creole vegetables. Reserve package of seasoning mix. Stir-fry about 1 minute. Add boiling broth. Blend and bring to a full boil. Add rice. Cover. Steam for 5 minutes, stirring occasionally. When rice is tender, stir in dissolved cornstarch. Stir until liquid has thickened. Sprinkle packaged seasoning mix over each serving. Makes 4 servings.

Note:

If mixed vegetables are used instead of New Orleans-style creole vegetables with seasoning packet, add 1/2 teaspoon mixed Italian herbs.

Flounder With Grapefruit

What a tasty and unusual blend!

4 (1/2-lb.) flounder fillets
3 tablespoons finely minced green onion
1 tablespoon finely minced fresh ginger
Salt and pepper to taste
1/2 cup dry white wine
2 tablespoons butter
2 cups whole grapefruit sections, well drained

Arrange fillets in shallow baking dish. Sprinkle with onion, ginger, salt and pepper. Pour wine over fillets and dot with butter. Surround with grapefruit sections. Place on rack in wok over simmering water. Cover wok and steam for 8 to 10 minutes or until fish flakes easily when touched with a fork. Serve immediately. Makes 4 servings.

Fish Fillets

Crisp and tender, drenched in garlic-lemon butter.

4 (6-oz.) fresh fish fillets, flounder, red snapper or trout
Flour, to dredge
2 tablespoons oil
4 tablespoons butter
1 clove garlic, peeled, finely minced
Salt and pepper to taste
1/2 cup minced parsley
1/4 cup fresh lemon juice
Lemon wedges, for garnish

Wash and dry the fish. Cut each in 1-1/2-inch pieces. Dredge each in flour, pressing flour evenly into fish, then shaking off excess. Heat wok. Add oil and butter. When butter melts and begins to sizzle add a few fish pieces at a time. Cook quickly over medium heat, turning until they are lightly browned on both sides. Remove and set aside. Add garlic to oil and butter. Stir-fry about 15 seconds. Remove wok from heat. Add fish, salt, pepper, parsley and lemon juice. Toss fish briefly in mixture. Garnish with lemon wedges. Makes 4 servings.

MEATS

We all enjoy meat. But, as you know, really good meat is almost out-of-sight expensive and even the so-called budget cuts are no longer cheap. This is one of the big reasons you'll appreciate wok meat cookery. Another reason is superb taste. You'll find that whether you braise it, stir-fry it or steam it, meat cooked in a wok costs less, portion for portion, than when it's prepared by any other method. Meat cooked in a wok does not shrink as it usually does when dry-roasted in your oven or broiled under high heat, and it retains all of its juicy goodness. You can stretch your budget even further when you use meat in a stir-fry dish—less meat can serve more people. For example, you can broil a one-pound steak to serve 2 people, or you can use that same steak in a stir-fry meat and vegetable dish that will serve 4 to 6 people.

In this section you'll find beef dishes in several languages, from Yankee Pot Roast, page 144, to Pronto Chili con Carne, page 185, to Beef Teriyaki, page 161. There are recipes in degrees of elegance from Briased Fillet of Beef, page 164, to Country-Style Ground-Beef Stew, page 162. Best of all, most combine meat and vegetables and, sometimes, potatoes, pasta or rice to make easy-on-the-cook, great-tasting, one-dish meals.

All meat for stir-fry dishes should be cut as thinly as possible or ground. If your butcher isn't cooperative about this, you can do it yourself. Raw meat slices easily if it's partially frozen. You do need a razor-sharp knife for this, so have yours sharpened if it has become dull.

Buy the best and leanest ground meat obtainable. Pound for pound, this pays off in savings. All too often what seems like bargain-priced hamburger has extra fat that has to be discarded. It's like pouring money down the drain. If you can persuade your butcher to grind the meat, pick a lean cut before it's ground to your order and ask that it not be packed down. Ground meat tastes far better if it is handled as little as possible.

Braising calls for a solid piece of meat, such as a good pot roast or a fillet of beef. Have it tied securely so that it will hold its shape while cooking. It's a good idea to buy a sufficiently large cut for planned leftovers. Sliced braised meat is ideal for many stir-fry dishes.

If you don't plan to use leftover meat within a day or two, slice and freeze it in meal-size portions. Place it in a freezer container and cover with leftover braising liquid that you have first chilled sufficiently to remove all fat.

EASY SOUTH-OF-THE-BORDER PARTY

Guacamole With Crackers
Taco Stir-Fry, page 180
Fresh Pineapple

DINNER A LA ROMA

Beef & Zucchini, page 170
Crusty Italian Rolls
Preserved Figs With Slivered Almonds
Strega Liqueur

DINNER WITH AN ITALIAN ACCENT

Veal & Peppers Romano, page 179
Crusty Italian Bread
Ripe Pears With Bel Paese Cheese
Espresso Coffee

Hawaiian Stir-Fry Ground Beef

An especially flavorful way to serve ground beef.

2 tablespoons oil
1 lb. lean ground round steak
1/4 cup chopped water chestnuts
1/4 cup chopped green onions
1 clove garlic, finely minced
1/4 cup candied ginger, finely chopped
1/4 cup beef broth
2 tablespoons soy sauce
1 egg, slightly beaten
2 cups hot cooked rice

Heat oil in wok. Add meat and stir-fry, until no longer pink.
Break up meat as it cooks. Add water chestnuts, onions,
garlic and ginger. Stir-fry for 2 to 3 minutes. Pour in broth.
Blend. Cover and steam for 1 minute. Stir in soy sauce.
Add egg and mix it into other ingredients. Serve over hot
cooked rice. Makes 4 to 6 servings.

Yankee Pot Roast

A juicy and tender roast.

1/3 lb. salt pork
1 (4- to 5-lb.) beef round, room temperature
All-purpose flour, to dredge
1/2 cup chopped onion
1/2 cup chopped carrot
1/4 cup chopped celery
1 clove garlic, peeled, minced
1 cup dry red wine
1 cup beef broth
1/2 teaspoon salt
1/2 teaspoon coarse-ground black pepper
1/4 teaspoon dried marjoram
1/4 teaspoon dried thyme
4 carrots, peeled, cut into 1-1/2- to 2-inch pieces
2 white turnips, peeled, quartered
6 to 8 small white onions, peeled

Rinse salt pork in cold water to remove excess salt. Blot dry and cut in small cubes. Place in wok over low heat. Cook, stirring often, until fat is rendered. Remove pork with slotted spoon and discard. Heat rendered fat over high heat. Blot meat dry; dredge with flour. Brown on all sides in hot fat. Remove meat and set aside. Add onion, carrot, celery and garlic to the wok. Cook over medium heat, stirring often, about 10 minutes. Add browned meat to vegetables. Add wine, broth, salt, pepper, marjoram and thyme. Bring to a boil and cover. Lower heat and simmer for 2 hours or until meat is almost tender. Add carrots, turnips and onions. Continue to simmer, covered, until meat and vegetables are tender. Place meat on a hot serving platter and surround with carrots, turnips and

Three-Star Vegetable Platter

Chicken Breasts Maryland

Sweet & Sour Shrimp

Corned Beef & Cabbage

East-West Stir-Fry

Chinese Fruited Pork

Pineapple Flan

Pears Cardinal

onions. Spoon some of the cooking liquid over meat and vegetables. Strain remaining liquid. Reheat if ncessary and serve separately or pour into storage jar and refrigerate for future use. Makes 6 to 8 servings.

Deviled Beef & Onions

A delicious way to use leftover pot roast.

1-1/2 to 2 cups leftover unthickened pot-roast gravy or
   1 (8-oz.) can beef gravy
2 to 3 teaspoons cornstarch
1 tablespoon soy sauce
1 teaspoon Worcestershire sauce
1 teaspoon prepared mustard
2 tablespoons brandy or sherry
2 tablespoons oil
1/4 teaspoon salt
3 medium mild purple onions, peeled, sliced thin
   and separated into rings
1-1/2 to 2 cups thin slices leftover beef pot roast
4 to 6 thick slices, French- or Italian-style bread

In a small bowl, combine gravy and cornstarch. Stir in soy sauce, Worcestershire sauce, mustard and brandy or sherry. Heat oil with salt in wok. Add onion rings and stir-fry for 1 minute or until soft. Add leftover pot-roast slices; stir in gravy. Stir until heated. Spoon over bread. Makes 4 to 6 servings.

Red Cooked Beef Chinese-Style

A different & delicious cold meat.

1/4 cup oil
1/2 teaspoon salt
2 to 2-1/2-lbs. boneless chuck or eye roast, room
   temperature
1 cup sherry
2 cloves garlic
1 (1-in.) cube fresh ginger, peeled
1 tablespoon sugar
Water
1/2 cup soy sauce
Hot Sauce, see below

Hot Sauce:

1 clove garlic, peeled, minced
1/2 cup cooking liquid from beef
1 (7-1/2-oz.) can jalapeño peppers
1 teaspoon sugar
Salt to taste

Heat oil with salt in wok over medium heat. Add meat and brown on all sides. Add sherry, garlic, ginger, sugar and enough water to almost cover meat. Bring to a boil; lower heat so liquid just simmers. Add soy sauce and cover. Simmer about 1-1/2 hours. Uncover and turn meat in liquid. Continue cooking for 1 hour or until meat is tender. Remove meat from stock. Let stand at room temperature about 15 minutes. Continue cooking stock until it is reduced by about half. Strain and use 1/2 cup for Hot Sauce. Cover cooled meat and refrigerate. Use remaining stock as liquid for stir-fry dishes. Slice meat and serve cold. Serve Hot Sauce separately. Makes 6 to 8 servings.

Hot Sauce:

Combine all ingredients in a small bowl. Stir until well blended.

Braised Beef Hash

Grated potatoes make a special hash.

4 baked potatoes, chilled
2 tablespoons oil
1 to 1-1/2 cups diced leftover cooked beef
4 tablespoons sour cream, room temperature
2 tablespoons Sauce Robert or thick steak sauce
Salt and pepper to taste

Peel potatoes and grate on the coarse side of grater; do not pack down. Heat oil in wok. Add potatoes and beef. Cook over high heat, stirring occasionally, until potatoes begin to brown. Remove from heat. In a small bowl, combine sour cream with Sauce Robert or thick steak sauce. Pour over meat and potatoes. Gently stir with fork to blend. Season with salt and pepper to taste. Makes 4 to 6 servings.

Boston Beef & Noodles

Rich tender beef in a superb one-dish supper.

1 (8-oz.) pkg. fine noodles
Water
1/4 teaspoon salt
Few drops of oil
1 cup cold water
2 teaspoons oil
2 tablespoons oil
1 lb. boneless sirloin or tenderloin of beef steak,
    cut across grain in thin strips
4 to 6 shallots, peeled, chopped
2 tablespoons sherry
1/2 cup beef broth
2 teaspoons Worcestershire sauce
2 teaspoons cornstarch dissolved in 2 tablespoons
    water
1 small head Boston lettuce, shredded
1 cup bean sprouts

Drop noodles into a large pot of rapidly boiling salted water. Add a few drops of oil. Cook until noodles rise to the surface and are pliable, about 1 minute. Immediately add 1 cup cold water and transfer contents into a colander. Drain, then transfer to a warm bowl. Add 2 teaspoons oil and toss to coat noodles evenly. Set aside. Heat 2 tablespoons oil in wok. Add beef strips. Stir-fry over high heat until no longer pink. Add shallots and stir-fry for 1 minute. Pour in sherry, broth and Worcestershire sauce. Cover and steam for 1 minute. Add dissolved cornstarch; stir until sauce thickens slightly. Add lettuce and bean sprouts. Stir-fry about 30 seconds. Stir in noodles. Stir and toss until heated. Makes 3 to 4 servings.

Deviled Steak in Pita Rolls

Your teenagers will adore these.

6 pita rolls (Arabic pocket bread)
1 tablespoon oil
1 lb. lean ground top-round steak
1 tablespoon Worcestershire sauce
1 tablespoon Dijon mustard
1 tablespoon prepared horseradish
2 tablespoons capers
2 teaspoons cornstarch dissolved in 2 tablespoons water
1/4 cup beef broth

Heat pita rolls and open one side. Heat oil in wok over high heat. Add beef and stir-fry until no longer pink. Stir in Worcestershire sauce, mustard, horseradish and capers. Stir dissolved cornstarch into beef broth. Add to meat and stir until liquid thickens. Spoon into pita rolls and serve hot. Makes 6 servings.

Hearty Creole Beef Stew

Fix it fast with economical cube steak.

About 3/4 cup flour
1 teaspoon salt
1/2 teaspoon pepper
1 teaspoon paprika
1-1/2 lbs. beef cube steak, cut in 2" x 2" squares
2 to 4 tablespoons oil

1 tablespoon oil
1 clove garlic, peeled, crushed
1/2 cup chopped celery
1/4 cup chopped green pepper
1/2 cup chopped onion
1 (11-1/2-oz.) can Italian-style tomatoes with basil
1 (8-oz.) can tomato sauce
1 cup cooked lima beans
1 cup cooked whole-kernel corn
2 to 3 dashes Tabasco® sauce
Salt and pepper to taste

In a small bowl mix flour, salt, pepper and paprika. Coat meat in flour mixture. Place on hard surface. With the flat side of a cleaver or a heavy rolling pin, pound coating into meat. Heat 2 tablespoons of oil in wok. Cook meat over high heat, a few pieces at a time, until well browned. Add more oil as needed. Remove meat and set aside. Add 1 tablespoon oil and garlic to wok. Stir garlic around sides of wok until lightly browned. Remove and discard garlic. Add celery, green pepper and onion. Stir-fry for 2 minutes. Return meat to wok. Add tomatoes, tomato sauce, lima beans and corn. Heat to boiling. Reduce heat, cover and let simmer for 5 minutes. Stir occasionally. Add Tabasco® sauce; season to taste with salt and pepper. Makes 6 servings.

Carne Asada

For a South-of-the-Border treat, serve this superb Mexican-style steak.

4 (1/4-lb.) New York-cut steaks, 1/4-in.-thick, sliced thin,
   room temperature
1/4 teaspoon salt
1/4 teaspoon pepper
1 tablespoon oil
1 large mild purple onion, peeled, cut in thin strips
   lengthwise
1 (7-1/2-oz.) can Mexican green-chili sauce

Trim fat from steaks and reserve. Rub salt and pepper into steaks. Heat oil in wok. Add onion and stir-fry until soft. Remove and set aside. Wipe wok clean with paper towel. Place over high heat. Add a 2-inch piece of the reserved fat. Holding it with a long-handled fork, move it around bottom and sides until wok is coated. Remove and discard fat. Add 1 steak. Cook for 1 minute on each side. Place on a heated platter. Repeat using reserved fat until all steaks are fried. Return onions to wok and add chili sauce. Stir until heated. Spoon a little over each steak. Serve remaining sauce separately. Makes 4 servings.

San Francisco Stir-Fry

East meets West in this beautiful blend.

2 tablespoons oil
1/2 teaspoon salt
1 clove garlic, peeled, crushed
3/4 lb. lean tenderloin of beef, about 1-1/2-in.-thick,
    cut across the grain into 1/8-in.-thick slices
1/2 cup chopped onion
1 cup finely shredded cabbage
1/4 cup beef broth
1 tablespoon soy sauce
1 (10-oz.) pkg. San Francisco-style frozen mixed
    vegetables with seasoning mix, partially thawed
1 tomato, cut into 8 thin strips, seeds and center pulp
    removed
1 teaspoon cornstarch dissolved in 1 tablespoon water
2 cups hot cooked rice
Fried Chinese noodles, packaged, for garnish
Soy sauce

Heat oil with salt in wok. Add garlic and stir-fry until
browned. Remove and discard. Add beef strips and stir-fry
until no longer pink; remove and set aside. Add onion and
cabbage and stir-fry for 1 minute. Pour in broth and soy
sauce. Bring liquid to a boil. Add partially thawed
vegetables; reserve package of seasoning mix. Stir broth-
vegetable mixture to blend. Cover. Steam 3 to 4 minutes or
until vegetables are tender. Add beef and tomato strips.
Stir-fry about 30 seconds. Add dissolved cornstarch and
continue stirring until thickened. Spoon over hot cooked
rice and sprinkle with seasoning mix from frozen
vegetables. Top with Chinese noodles. Serve with soy
sauce at the table. Makes 4 servings.

Short Ribs of Beef Southern-Style

Tasty, lean short ribs with sweet potatoes on the side.

Water
1-1/2 lbs. short ribs of beef
2 large sweet potatoes
1/2 cup catsup
1 tablespoon Worcestershire sauce
2 tablespoons light-brown sugar
2 tablespoons cider vinegar
1 teaspoon salt

Pour water into wok to bottom of rack. Bring to simmer. Place meat on rack. Cover and steam for 1 hour. Add sweet potatoes to rack. Cover and continue steaming for 30 minutes or until meat is tender. Remove meat and potatoes from wok. Set potatoes aside. Cut fat from meat and discard fat. Place meat in a long shallow baking dish that will fit into wok. Combine remaining ingredients, pour over meat. Place dish in wok over simmering water. Place partially cooked potatoes on rack on each side of meat dish. Cover and steam for 30 minutes. Baste meat with sauce occasionally. If potatoes are cooked before meat, remove them, cut in half and keep warm. Makes 4 servings.

Stir-Fry Beef & Corn Mexican-Style

Here's what to do with leftover Texas Barbecued Braised Beef, page 156.

2 tablespoons oil
1/2 teaspoon salt
1/2 cup diced green pepper
2 cups whole-kernel corn, frozen or canned
1/4 cup diced pimiento, well drained
1 tomato, cut in wedges
2 cups leftover diced Texas Barbecued
   Braised Beef, page 156
1 tablespoon chili sauce
1/2 cup fat-free leftover gravy from Texas Barbecued
   Braised Beef, page 156
1 small head Boston lettuce, torn into bite-size chunks
1/2 cup chopped onion

Heat oil with salt in wok. Add green pepper and stir-fry for 1 minute. Add corn, pimiento, tomato and diced meat. Stir-fry until heated. In a small bowl combine chili sauce and gravy. Stir into vegetable-meat mixture. Bring to a boil and add lettuce. Stir-fry for 15 seconds. Top each serving with chopped onion. Makes 4 servings.

Steak Diane

Cook it right at the table for a spectacular effect!

2 tablespoons oil
2 (1-1/2-lb.) filet mignon, (1-1/2-in. thick) pounded
   1-in. thick
2 tablespoons butter
1/4 cup minced green onions, white part only, or shallots
3 tablespoons brandy
1 tablespoon minced parsley
1 tablespoon minced chives, if desired
2 tablespoons Worcestershire sauce
2 tablespoons Sauce Diable or 1 teaspoon
   Worcestershire sauce and 1 teaspoon
   prepared mustard
2 slices thin crisp toast

Heat oil in wok. Brown the filets quickly over high heat.
Place on a heated platter. Add butter to wok. Stir-fry green
onions or shallots in butter over low heat until limp. Return
the filets to the wok. Turn heat to high. Pour in brandy.
Warm and ignite. When flame dies add remaining
ingredients and cook for 1 to 2 minutes. Serve at once
over thin crisp toast. Makes 2 servings.

Tokyo-Style Stir-Fry

Economical cube steak and convenient frozen vegetables make this memorable meal.

2 tablespoons oil
1/2 teaspoon salt
6 large mushrooms, trimmed and sliced thinly through stems
1 medium green pepper, seeded and cut in strips
1 lb. lean cube steak, trimmed and cut in narrow strips
1/2 cup water
1 (10-oz.) pkg. frozen Japanese-style stir-fry vegetables with seasoning mix, partially thawed
2 to 3 cups hot cooked rice

Heat oil and salt in wok. Add mushrooms and stir-fry for 1 minute. Add green-pepper strips and continue to stir-fry for 1 minute. Add meat strips and stir-fry until no longer pink, about 1 minute. Add water and bring to a boil. Stir in partially thawed vegetables and seasoning mix. Return to boil. Cover, lower heat and simmer for 3 minutes. Serve over hot cooked rice. Makes 4 to 6 servings.

Corned Beef & Cabbage

And for dessert serve Old-Fashioned Deep-Fried Apple Pies, page 256.

1 (2- to 2-1/2-lb.) corned brisket of beef
6 to 8 small new potatoes, washed, unpeeled
1 small cabbage, washed in salt water, rinsed, quartered
Hot mustard, for garnish
Sweet-pickle chips, for garnish

Place brisket directly on rack in wok over simmering water. Cover and steam for 45 minutes per pound or until meat can be easily pierced with a fork. Add new potatoes the last 30 minutes of steaming. Place brisket on a serving platter. Let stand 15 to 20 minutes before carving. Remove potatoes when tender and add cabbage to rack. Cover and steam cabbage for 10 to 15 minutes or until crisp-tender. Arrange sliced meat on platter. Surround with potatoes and cabbage wedges. Serve with mustard and sweet-pickle chips. Makes 4 servings.

Ground-Beef Diable With Fried Noodles

You'll enjoy this ground beef with a different taste.

1 lb. lean ground beef
1/4 cup sherry
2 tablespoons Sauce Diable or
    1 teaspoon Worcestershire sauce and

1 teaspoon prepared mustard
1 teaspoon salt
2 tablespoons cornstarch
1 cup oil for deep frying
4 oz. uncooked fine noodles
1/2 cup chopped onion
1/4 cup chopped green pepper
1 cup beef broth
2 teaspoons cornstarch dissolved in 2 tablespoons water
2 to 3 cups hot cooked noodles or rice

In a bowl mix ground beef with sherry, Sauce Diable or Worcestershire sauce with mustard, and salt and cornstarch. Heat oil in wok to 375°F (191°C) or until a 1-inch cube of bread browns in 50 to 60 seconds. Add fine noodles and deep-fry for 3 minutes or until golden brown. Drain noodles and place in a deep dish. Pour oil from wok. Reserve 2 tablespoons oil and return to wok. Place wok over high heat. Add onion and green pepper. Stir-fry for 1 minute. Add meat mixture. Continue cooking until meat is lightly browned. Add broth, stir in dissolved cornstarch and bring to a boil. Stir until slightly thickened. Pour over the fried noodles. Toss and serve with hot cooked soft noodles or hot cooked rice. Makes 4 to 6 servings.

Texas Barbecued Braised Beef

From deep in the heart of Texas.

1 (3- to 3-1/2-lb.) top round of beef, boned and tied
2 tablespoons oil
1 clove garlic, peeled and minced

2 small white onions, peeled and chopped
1 (7-1/2-oz.) can jalapeño relish
2 cups water
1 teaspoon salt
1/2 teaspoon pepper
2 teaspoons chili powder

Bring meat to room temperature. Blot dry with paper towel. Heat oil in wok over high heat. Add meat and brown well on both sides. Turn with Chinese ladle and spatula or 2 wooden spoons to prevent piercing meat. Remove meat and set aside. Add garlic and onions to wok. Stir-fry until soft. Add meat and remaining ingredients. Bring to a boil. Lower heat and cover. Simmer for 45 minutes per pound or until meat is tender. Remove meat from liquid. Let stand for 10 to 15 minutes before slicing. Slice and serve with a little of the cooking liquid spooned over each slice. If desired, use leftover beef and gravy to make Stir-Fry Beef & Corn Mexican-Style, page 154. Makes 6 to 8 servings.

Beef With Broccoli & Curried Rice

Your butcher can slice the meat paper-thin on his electric slicer.

1 small bunch broccoli, about 1 lb.
2 tablespoons oil
1 lb. lean sirloin of beef (about 1-1/2-in. thick), sliced very thin
2 tablespoons oil
1/2 teaspoon salt
1/2 cup chopped onion

1 teaspoon curry powder
2-3/4 cup water
1 (7-oz.) pkg. curried-rice mix
1 (8-oz.) can water chestnuts, drained and thinly sliced

Trim and cut broccoli stems. Break tops into bite-size flowerets. Cut stems lengthwise into 1/8-inch-thick by 1-inch-long "matchsticks." Heat 2 tablespoons of oil in wok. Add beef slices. Stir-fry over high heat until no longer pink; remove and set aside. Add remaining 2 tablespoons oil and salt to wok. Add onion, curry powder and broccoli; stir-fry for 1 minute. Add 1/4 cup of water. Cover and steam for 1 minute. Uncover and stir-fry until liquid evaporates and vegetables are tender; remove and set aside. Add remaining water to wok. Bring to boil, add rice mix and stir-fry 1 minute. Lower heat and cover. Steam for 25 minutes or until liquid is absorbed and rice is tender. Add water chestnuts, broccoli, onion and beef. Stir until heated. Makes 4 to 6 servings.

Beef With Peanuts

Sweet and salty, crunchy and tender—try this delightful blend of flavors and textures.

2 tablespoons oil
1/2 teaspoon salt
1 lb. ground round steak
1 (10-oz.) pkg. frozen peas, partially thawed
1 teaspoon sugar
2 tablespoons sherry

1/3 cup chicken broth or water
1 tablespoon soy sauce
1 cup bean sprouts
1 tablespoon cornstarch dissolved in 2 tablespoons
  water
1/2 cup dry-roasted peanuts
2 to 3 cups hot cooked rice

Heat oil with salt in wok. Add ground meat and stir-fry over high heat until no longer pink. Add peas and stir-fry for 30 seconds. Sprinkle with sugar. Add sherry and cook, stirring for 1 minute. Add broth or water and cover. Steam for 2 to 3 minutes, stirring occasionally. When peas are tender, add soy sauce and bean sprouts. Add dissolved cornstarch and stir until thickened. Stir in peanuts. Serve over hot cooked rice. Makes 4 to 6 servings.

Beef Teriyaki

Sweet soy-sauce flavor with a touch of ginger.

2 lbs. flank steak, cut diagonally across grain in
  thin strips
1 medium onion, peeled and chopped
1 clove garlic, peeled and split lengthwise
1 (1-in.) cube fresh ginger, crushed
2 tablespoons sugar
1/2 cup soy sauce
1/2 cup sherry
2 tablespoons oil
2 teaspoons cornstarch dissolved in 1 tablespoon water
2 cups hot cooked rice

Place steak slices in a large non-metal bowl. Cover with onion, garlic, ginger and sugar. Combine soy sauce and sherry. Pour over meat mixture. Let stand at room temperature for 2 to 3 hours. Remove beef strips. Drain and blot dry. Strain marinade and set aside. Heat oil in wok over high heat. Stir-fry beef strips a few at a time until lightly browned. Place on a hot platter. Add strained marinade to wok and bring to a boil. Add dissolved cornstarch and stir until liquid thickens. Pour over steak strips and serve over hot cooked rice. Makes 4 to 6 servings.

Country-Style Ground-Beef Stew

Down-home flavor in minutes.

1 tablespoon oil
1 lb. ground chuck beef
1/4 cup chopped onion
1/4 cup chopped green pepper
2 (1-lb.) cans tomatoes
1 (10-oz.) pkg. frozen whole-kernel corn
4 oz. flat noodles
1/4 cup beef broth or water, if needed
1/2 cup sliced pimiento-stuffed olives
1 cup shredded milk Cheddar cheese
Salt to taste

Heat oil in wok. Add beef. Stir-fry until lightly browned. Pour off any excess fat. Add onion and green pepper. Continue to stir-fry about 1 minute. Add tomatoes. Chop and break up. Cover. Simmer for ten minutes, stirring occasionally. Add corn. Cover and steam for 5 minutes. Add noodles and simmer uncovered until tender. Add a little broth or water if mixture becomes dry. Mix in olives and cheese. Continue stirring until cheese melts and stew thickens. Salt to taste. Makes 6 servings.

Steak With Mushrooms

Tiny steak pieces stir-fried in a tasty sauce.

1-1/2 lbs. shell or club steak trimmed and boned
2 tablespoons soy sauce
1 tablespoon Worcestershire sauce
2 tablespoons sherry
1 teaspoon sugar
2 teaspoons cornstarch
1/2 teaspoon black pepper
1 teaspoon sesame oil or peanut oil
1/2 cup oil
1/2 lb. mushrooms, coarsely chopped
4 green onions, cut in 1-in. lengths
1 (8-oz.) can bamboo shoots, drained
1 (10-oz.) pkg. frozen snow peas, thawed
3 tablespoons water

Cut steaks in 1-1/2-inch cubes. Pound each cube on all sides using a mallet or the flat side of a heavy cleaver. Place meat in a bowl. Add soy sauce, Worcestershire sauce, sherry, sugar, cornstarch, pepper and 1 teaspoon sesame oil or peanut oil. Stir well; let stand for 30 minutes. Heat 1/2 cup oil in wok over high heat. Add meat and stir-fry about 2 minutes. Remove and drain steak. Pour oil from wok, reserving 2 tablespoons. Add mushrooms and green onions and stir-fry for 2 minutes. Add bamboo shoots and snow peas. Stir-fry for 30 seconds. Return meat to wok. Add water and continue to cook, stirring for 30 seconds. Makes 4 servings.

Braised Fillet of Beef

This luxurious cut has a special vegetable sauce.

1/4 lb. salt pork
1 (3-1/2- to 4-lb.) fillet of beef, room temperature
1/2 cup finely diced carrots
1 cup chopped green onions
1 cup chopped celery
Salt and pepper to taste
1/2 cup water or beef broth

Rinse salt pork in cold water to remove excess salt. Blot dry and cut in small cubes. Heat wok to medium. Stir-fry salt pork until fat has been rendered and pork cubes are crisp and brown. Remove pork with slotted spoon and discard. Brown fillet on all sides in rendered fat over high heat. Remove and set aside. Add carrots, onions and celery to remaining fat in wok. Stir-fry until limp. Place fillet in wok directly over vegetables; sprinkle with salt and pepper. Add water or broth and cover. Braise over medium heat for 30 to 35 minutes for rare, 40 to 45 minutes for medium. Place on a serving platter. Allow to stand for 10 to 15 minutes before slicing. Serve hot or cold. Makes 6 to 8 servings.

Stir-Fry Corned Beef & Cabbage

A new approach to a traditional dish.

2 tablespoons oil
1/2 teaspoon salt
1 small cabbage, shredded (about 4 cups)
1 small white onion, peeled, finely chopped
1 medium tart apple, peeled, cored and chopped
1/4 cup water
1 teaspoon sugar
1 (1-lb.) can corned beef, coarsely chopped
2 tablespoons soy sauce
2 teaspoons cornstarch dissolved in 2 tablespoons water

Heat oil with salt in wok. Add cabbage, onion and apple. Stir-fry for 2 minutes. Add water and sugar. Cover and steam about 10 minutes or until cabbage is still slightly crisp. Uncover and stir occasionally. Add corned beef. Stir-fry for 1 minute. Cover and steam about 1 to 2 minutes or until corned beef is heated. Add soy sauce and dissolved cornstarch. Stir until slightly thickened. Makes 4 to 6 servings.

Sweet & Sour Meatballs

Brussels sprouts really add flavor.

1 lb. lean ground beef
1 cup soft bread crumbs
1 egg, slightly beaten
1/4 teaspoon salt
1/4 teaspoon ground coriander
2 tablespoons prepared horseradish
Cornstarch
1/2 cup oil
1 (10-oz.) pkg. frozen Brussels sprouts
1 tablespoon oil
1 clove garlic, peeled, crushed
1/4 cup chopped onion
1 (8-1/2-oz.) can water chestnuts
1 (15-1/2-oz.) can unsweetened pineapple chunks,
   drained; reserve 1/2 cup juice
Sweet & Sour Sauce, see below
2 cups hot cooked rice

Sweet & Sour Sauce:

1/3 cup sugar
1/3 cup cider vinegar
2 tablespoons soy sauce
2 tablespoons sherry
1/4 cup tomato sauce or catsup
2 tablespoons cornstarch dissolved in 1/2 cup
   reserved pineapple juice (from canned pineapple
   chunks)

In a large bowl, combine beef with bread crumbs, egg, salt, coriander and horseradish. Mix thoroughly. Shape into 8 small balls. Roll each in cornstarch. Heat oil in wok to

375°F (191°C). Fry meatballs, a few at a time, until browned. Remove and set aside. Drain oil from wok. Place frozen Brussels sprouts in a shallow baking dish on rack in wok over simmering water. Cover and steam for 5 minutes or until tender. Set aside. Drain and dry wok. Heat 1 tablespoon of oil in wok. Add garlic and fry until browned; remove and discard. Add onion and stir-fry for 30 seconds. Reduce heat. Add Brussels sprouts, meatballs, water chestnuts and pineapple chunks. Pour in Sweet & Sour Sauce. Stir until heated. Serve over hot cooked rice. Makes 4 servings.

Sweet & Sour Sauce:

Combine all ingredients in saucepan. Cook over medium heat, stirring, until sauce is thickened. Remove from heat and set aside.

How to Make
Sweet & Sour Meatballs

Shape ground-meat mixture into 8 balls. Roll each ball in cornstarch.

Combine ingredients for Sweet & Sour Sauce. Place in a saucepan and cook over medium heat until sauce thickens. Set aside.

After frying meatballs in hot oil, combine with onion, steamed Brussels sprouts, water chestnuts and pineapple. Add sauce and stir until mixture is heated through.

Serve Sweet & Sour meatballs over hot cooked rice.

Beef & Zucchini

Easy, fast and great tasting. Nutritious, too.

1 tablespoon oil
1 clove garlic, peeled, minced
1/2 cup chopped onion
1 lb. lean ground beef
3 medium zucchini, trimmed, sliced at a 45-degree
    angle into thin ovals
1 large ripe tomato, chopped
2 tablespoons water, more if needed
Salt to taste
Coarse-ground black pepper to taste
1/2 cup grated Parmesan cheese
Italian-style bread or cooked flat noodles
Grated Parmesan cheese, if desired

Heat wok. Add oil, garlic and onion. Stir-fry over medium heat until limp. Add ground beef and continue to stir until meat is no longer pink. Stir in zucchini and tomato. Add water. Season to taste with salt and pepper. Cover and steam until zucchini is tender. Stir occasionally. Add additional water if mixture becomes dry. Stir in 1/2 cup grated cheese. Serve with bread or over flat noodles. Serve additional grated cheese at the table. Makes 4 servings.

Hungarian Ground-Beef Goulash

Hearty family fare.

1 (10-oz.) pkg. frozen mixed stewed vegetables,
   partially thawed
2 tablespoons oil
1/2 teaspoon salt
1/4 cup chopped green onion
1 lb. lean ground beef
1 tablespoon imported Hungarian paprika
1 cup beef broth, more if needed
2 teaspoons cornstarch
3/4 cup sour cream
1 tablespoon tomato paste

Cut potatoes in package of frozen vegetables in bite-size
pieces. Heat oil with salt in wok. Add onion and stir-fry over
high heat until soft. Add beef and stir-fry until lightly
browned. Drain any excess fat. Stir in paprika. Pour in
broth and bring to a boil. Add partially thawed stew
vegetables. Reduce heat. Cover and simmer about 20
minutes, or until vegetables are cooked. Stir frequently.
Add a little more broth if necessary to keep vegetables
half-covered with liquid. Stir cornstarch into sour cream.
Add tomato paste and mix well. Stir into goulash. Continue
stirring and heat thoroughly, but do not boil. Makes 4 to 6
servings.

Lamb With White Beans

A truly delectable stir-fry dish.

2 tablespoons butter
1 tablespoon oil
1 medium mild onion, peeled, chopped
1 clove garlic, peeled, minced
1 (1-lb.) can whole tomatoes, drained; reserve 1/2 cup
  juice
1/2 cup reserved tomato juice
1/4 teaspoon thyme
1/2 teaspoon salt
1/4 teaspoon pepper
2 teaspoons cornstarch dissolved in 2 tablespoons water
2 to 2-1/2 cups cooked White Beans with Tomato &
  Garlic, page 76
1 to 1-1/2 cups cubed cooked roast lamb
2 to 3 tablespoons minced parsley

Heat butter and oil in wok over medium heat. Add onion
and garlic. Stir-fry until tender. Add tomatoes, tomato
juice, thyme, salt and pepper. Stir in dissolved cornstarch.
Add beans and lamb. Stir until heated and liquid slightly
thickens. Stir in parsley just before serving. Makes 4 to 6
servings.

Braised Veal With Vegetables

Sauce as tasty as any served in a French restaurant.

1 (3- to 4-lb.) rib roast of veal, boned, tied
1 clove garlic, peeled, slivered

2 tablespoons butter
8 large mushroom caps, reserve stems
5 tablespoons oil
1 cup chopped green onions
Chopped stems from 8 mushrooms
1/4 cup dry white wine
1-1/4 cups beef broth
Salt and pepper to taste
1 large tomato, quartered
8 small white onions, peeled
6 small carrots, peeled, cut in 2-in. pieces

Bring the meat to room temperature. Make slits along the length with a small sharp knife. Insert garlic slivers deep into meat. Heat butter in wok. Stir-fry mushroom caps in butter about 5 minutes. Remove and set aside. Pour 3 tablespoons of the oil in wok, over high heat. Add veal and brown well. Remove and set aside. Pour off oil and wipe wok clean with paper towel. Add remaining 2 tablespoons oil, green onions and mushroom stems. Stir-fry about 5 minutes. Push onions and mushroom stems together on bottom of wok and place browned veal on top. Pour in wine and broth. Sprinkle meat with salt and pepper to taste. Add tomato. Bring to a boil. Lower heat. Cover and simmer for about 1-1/2 hours, turning meat occasionally. Add white onions, carrots and sauteed mushroom caps. Continue to cook, covered, until vegetables and meat are tender, 1/2- to 1 hour more. Makes 6 servings.

Variation:

For a more delicate flavor, substitute chicken broth for beef broth.

Veal With Snow Peas & Water Chestnuts

A low-calorie treat.

1-1/2 cups thin strips Braised Veal, page 101
1/4 cup dry sherry
1/2 teaspoon sesame oil
2 tablespoons oil
1 clove garlic, peeled, minced
1 (10-oz.) pkg. snow peas with water chestnuts,
  thawed and drained
3/4 cup chicken broth
2 teaspoons cornstarch, dissolved in 2 tablespoons
  water
2 cups cooked rice

Place veal strips in a bowl. Add sherry and sesame oil. Let stand at room temperature for 10 to 15 minutes. Heat oil in wok. Add garlic and stir-fry about 2 minutes. Remove and discard garlic. Add snow peas and water chestnuts. Stir-fry for 1 minute. Add chicken broth and veal strips with sherry and sesame oil. Continue stirring about 1 minute. Stir in dissolved cornstarch. Stir until liquid thickens. Serve over rice. Makes 4 servings.

Variation:

Chicken or beef may be substituted for veal.

East-West Stir-Fry

A delightful Oriental flavor.

1 lb. lean ground beef
3 tablespoons oil
1/2 cup chopped onion
1/2 cup diagonally sliced celery
1 medium carrot, peeled, cut in paper-thin strips
   with vegetable peeler
1/4 lb. fresh green beans, trimmed, sliced lengthwise
1 small white turnip, peeled, thinly sliced through stems
4 large fresh mushrooms, trimmed, thinly sliced
   through stems
1/2 cup chicken broth
1 tablespoon honey
1/4 cup soy sauce
1 tablespoon cornstarch dissolved in 2 tablespoons
   water
1 (10-oz.) pkg. fresh spinach, washed, stemmed
3 cups cooked hot rice
Chopped dry-roasted peanuts, if desired

Shape beef into 1 large patty. Heat 1 tablespoon of the oil in wok over high heat. Add beef patty and brown for 2 to 2-1/2 minutes on each side. Break meat into chunks and stir-fry for 30 seconds. Remove and set aside. Pour remaining 2 tablespoons oil into wok. When sizzling, add onion, celery, carrot, green beans, turnip and mushrooms. Stir-fry for 2 minutes. Pour in broth and reduce heat. Cover and steam for 2 to 3 minutes. Stir occasionally. Stir in honey, soy sauce and dissolved cornstarch. Return meat to wok. Place spinach on top of meat and vegetables. Cover and steam for 1 minute. Uncover and stir spinach into sauce. Serve over hot cooked rice. If desired, sprinkle each serving with chopped peanuts. Makes 4 to 6 servings.

Curried Lamb With Peas

Tomatoes add color to this spicy Middle-Eastern meal.

1 tablespoon oil
1 large onion, peeled, chopped
1 tablespoon curry powder
1 lb. lean ground lamb
1/2 teaspoon salt
1 (1-lb.) can Italian-style peeled tomatoes
1 tablespoon tomato paste
2 tablespoons Mango Chutney, page 207
1 (10-oz.) pkg. frozen peas
Salt and pepper to taste
2 cups cooked rice or
    6 pita rolls (Arabic pocket bread)

Heat oil in wok. Add onion, stir-fry about 1 minute. Stir in curry powder. Add lamb and stir-fry, breaking up meat. Cook until no longer pink. Add salt and tomatoes. Stir in tomato paste. Cover and steam for 10 minutes, stirring often. Finely chop large pieces of mango in chutney. Add peas and chutney to wok; stir to blend. Cover and continue cooking until peas are tender, about 10 minutes. Season with salt and pepper to taste. Serve over rice or spoon into heated, split pita rolls. Makes 4 servings.

Hot Meat Turnovers

The Spanish name for these delicious meat pies is empañadas.

6 frozen patty shells
2 tablespoons oil
1/2 cup chopped onion
1 lb. lean ground beef
2 tablespoons flour
1 (8-oz.) can tomatoes, drained and mashed
1/2 cup sherry
1/4 cup chopped parsley
1 teaspoon dried dill
1 teaspoon salt
1/2 teaspoon paprika
1/4 teaspoon pepper
Oil for deep frying
1 (8-oz.) can beef gravy
1/4 cup dry sherry
1 tablespoon Sauce Diable or
    1 teaspoon Worcestershire sauce and
    1 teaspoon prepared mustard

Thaw frozen patty shells at room temperature. Heat oil in wok. Add onions and stir-fry until soft. Add beef, stir-frying until no longer pink. Stir in flour and tomatoes. Add sherry and stir until liquid thickens. Remove from heat. Add parsley, dill, salt, paprika and pepper. Mix thoroughly. On lightly floured surface, roll thawed cold patty shells, one at a time, into a circle about 3 times the original size. Spoon some of the meat mixture on one side of the circle. Moisten edges lightly with water and fold over. Press edges together with the tines of a fork. You can prepare these to this point and freeze them. If you do freeze the turnovers before frying, allow to stand at room temperature until pastry is soft, but still cold. Pour oil in wok to 3-inch depth in center. Heat to 375°F (191°C). Fry turnovers 2 at a time until lightly browned. Drain on paper towel. In a small saucepan combine beef gravy with sherry and Sauce Diable or Worcestershire sauce with mustard. Cook, stirring until heated. Just before serving, spoon a little over each turnover. Makes 6 turnovers.

Lamb With Tomatoes & Rice Oriental

Try this when you have leftover lamb.

2 tablespoons oil
2 to 3 cups cold cooked rice
1/2 cup slivered almonds
1/2 cup seedless raisins
2 tablespoons soy sauce
2 tablespoons oil
1/2 teaspoon salt
1 to 2 cups cooked chopped lean lamb
1 clove garlic, peeled, minced
1/4 cup chopped green onions
1/4 cup finely minced parsley
1 teaspoon grated lemon peel
1 tomato, seeded and cut in thin strips
Lemon wedges, for garnish

Heat 2 tablespoons oil in wok. Add rice and stir-fry over high heat until grains are coated. Stir in almonds, raisins and soy sauce. Cook, stirring about 30 seconds. Scrape contents of wok onto a heated platter. Wipe wok with paper towel. Add 2 tablespoons oil and salt. Place over high heat. Add lamb, garlic, onions, parsley and lemon peel. Stir-fry about 2 to 3 minutes. Add tomato strips and continue to cook, stirring about 1 minute. Tomato strips should be barely cooked. Spoon over rice. Serve with lemon wedges. Makes 4 to 6 servings.

Veal & Peppers Romano

Memories of a Roman holiday.

1/4 cup flour
1/2 teaspoon salt
1/4 teaspoon coarse-ground black pepper
1/2 lb. lean boneless veal, pounded thin, cut into
   3/4- to 1-in. strips
2 medium green peppers, seeded, cut into 1/2-in. strips,
   lengthwise
Water
2 tablespoons oil
2 medium tomatoes, cut in wedges
4 to 5 green onions, chopped
1 clove garlic, peeled, minced
1/2 cup chicken broth
1/2 teaspoon mixed Italian herbs
1/2 teaspoon salt
1/4 teaspoon pepper
2 cups cooked rice or noodles
Grated Romano or Parmesan cheese

Combine flour, salt and pepper. Rub mixture firmly into each strip of veal, shake off excess. In a saucepan, cover pepper strips with water. Bring to a boil. Lower heat, simmer for 5 minutes. Drain. Heat oil in wok. Add veal, tomatoes, green onions, garlic and pepper strips. Stir-fry about 2 minutes. Add broth, Italian herbs, salt and pepper. Stir, cover and steam for 5 minutes. Uncover and stir-fry about 2 to 3 minutes. Serve over rice or noodles. Sprinkle each serving with grated cheese. Makes 3 to 4 servings.

Variation:

Serve with Italian bread instead of rice or noodles. Makes 2 to 3 servings.

Taco Stir-Fry

Serve over crisp lettuce and garnish with avocado.

1 tablespoon oil
1 lb. lean ground beef
1/4 cup chopped onion
2 tablespoons chili powder or to taste
1 cup whole-kernel corn, canned or frozen
1 (1-lb.) can stewed tomatoes
1 teaspoon sugar
1/2 teaspoon dried crushed oregano
1/4 teaspoon salt
1/8 teaspoon pepper
1 cup chopped mild Cheddar cheese
1 (9-1/2-oz.) pkg. corn chips
2 small heads Boston lettuce, shredded
1 avocado, peeled, seeded and sliced, for garnish

Heat oil in wok. Add beef and onion. Stir-fry over high heat until beef is no longer pink and onion softens. Drain excess fat. Stir in chili powder, corn, tomatoes, sugar, oregano, salt and pepper. Bring to a boil. Lower heat. Cover and simmer about 10 minutes. Stir in cheese and corn chips. Cook, stirring until cheese is partially melted. Spoon over shredded lettuce. Garnish with avocado slices. Makes 6 servings.

Down-East Stir-Fry

Tiny new potatoes teamed with succulent veal strips.

8 small new potatoes
Water
2 tablespoons oil
1/2 teaspoon salt
8 large mushrooms, trimmed, sliced thin lengthwise
　　through stem
1/4 cup sauce from Braised Veal, page 170, or
　　chicken broth
1 (10-oz.) pkg. frozen New England-Style mixed
　　vegetables, with seasoning mix, partially thawed
1-1/2 cups strips of Braised Veal, page 170
1 teaspoon cornstarch dissolved in 1 tablespoon water

Steam potatoes on rack in wok over simmering water until tender. Peel and keep warm in a covered dish or in a 200°F (93°C) oven. Drain wok. Dry with paper towel. Heat oil with salt in wok. Add mushrooms and stir-fry about 1 minute. Add sauce or broth. Bring to a boil. Add partially thawed vegetables; reserve seasoning mix. Cover and steam for 4 minutes. Add veal and potatoes. Stir until heated. Add dissolved cornstarch and stir until sauce thickens. Sprinkle with seasoning mix from package of frozen vegetables. Makes 4 servings.

Special Deviled Beef With Beans

A frankly extravagant dish—but worth it.

1 tablespoon oil
3/4 lb. fillet of beef (1-in.-thick), cut in 1/2-in. strips
1 small white onion, peeled, minced
2 tablespoons cognac or brandy
1 (1-lb.) can imported flageolets or
   2 cups cooked White Beans With Tomato & Garlic,
   page 76
2 tablespoons Sauce Diable or
   1 teaspoon Worcestershire sauce and
   1 teaspoon prepared mustard
1 teaspoon Worcestershire sauce
2 to 3 dashes Tabasco® sauce
1/4 cup minced parsley
Salt to taste
Coarse-ground black pepper to taste

Heat oil in wok and add beef. Stir-fry until lightly browned.
Add onion and stir-fry for 1 minute. Pour in cognac or
brandy. Continue to cook, stirring for 2 minutes. Add
beans. Stir in remaining ingredients. Stir-fry 1 minute.
Makes 2 servings.

Deviled Beef With Noodles

A great way to cook inexpensive flank steak.

1 (8-oz.) pkg. fine noodles
Water
1/4 teaspoon salt
Few drops of oil
2 teaspoons oil
1 lb. flank steak, thinly sliced across the grain and
    finely shredded
1 teaspoon Worcestershire sauce
1 tablespoon cornstarch
3 tablespoons oil
1/2 teaspoon sugar
1/2 teaspoon salt
1/2 cup chicken broth
1 tablespoon Sauce Diable or
    1 teaspoon Worcestershire sauce and
    1 teaspoon prepared mustard

Drop noodles into a large pot of rapidly boiling salted
water. Add a few drops of oil. Cook until noodles rise to the
surface and are pliable, about 1 minute. Drain. Place in a
bowl and toss with 2 teaspoons oil. Place the shredded
beef in a second bowl. Add Worcestershire sauce, cornstarch and 1 tablespoon of the oil. Rub meat with fingers
to work mixture in evenly. Let stand about 15 minutes.
Heat remaining 2 tablespoons oil in wok. Add the meat
and stir-fry over high heat until no longer pink. Sprinkle
with sugar and salt. Push the meat to one side and add the
noodles. Stir-fry 30 seconds, then mix with the meat. Add
the broth. Bring to a boil. Stir in the Sauce Diable or
Worcestershire sauce with mustard. Stir about 30 seconds
and serve hot. Makes 4 to 6 servings.

Pronto Chili con Carne

Chili afficionados love this one.

1 tablespoon flour
1/2 cup cold water
1 tablespoon oil
1/2 cup chopped onion
1 lb. lean ground beef
1 tablespoon chili powder or to taste
1 (1-lb.) can stewed tomatoes
1 (15-oz.) can red kidney beans in tomato sauce
Salt to taste
Tortillas or hero rolls
1 cup grated Monterey Jack or Cheddar cheese

Mix flour into cold water and stir until smooth. Set aside. Heat oil in wok. Add onion; stir-fry until soft. Add meat and stir-fry until no longer pink. Drain excess rendered fat. Add chili powder, tomatoes and beans. Bring to a boil. Lower heat, cover and simmer about 10 minutes. Stir in flour-water mixture. Simmer until sauce thickens. Season with salt to taste. Serve over heated tortillas, or in split toasted hero rolls. Top with grated cheese. Makes 6 to 8 servings.

Beef-Stuffed Eggplant

Mango chutney is the secret ingredient.

1 medium eggplant, about 1-1/2 lbs.
Water
2 tablespoons oil
1 clove garlic, peeled, crushed
1/4 cup finely chopped green pepper
1/4 cup finely chopped onion
1/2 lb. lean ground beef
1/2 teaspoon salt
1/4 teaspoon pepper
1 teaspoon paprika
1/2 cup chicken broth
1 tablespoon Mango Chutney, page 207
1 egg, slightly beaten
8 crisp saltine crackers, finely crushed
Paprika

Using a 2-pronged fork, pierce eggplant skin in several places. Place on rack in wok over simmering water. Cover and steam for 20 to 25 minutes, or until eggplant is tender. Cut eggplant in half and let stand at room temperature until cool enough to handle. Scoop out the soft pulp. Gently pull strips of pulp away from skin, being careful to leave shells intact. Set shells aside. Chop pulp. Heat oil in wok. Add garlic. Stir-fry until lightly browned. Discard garlic. Add green pepper, onion and beef. Stir-fry until onion is soft and meat is no longer pink. Break up meat as it fries. Add salt, pepper, paprika and pulp. Stir seasoning into meat. Add broth and cover. Steam for 1 minute. Uncover and stir-fry until all liquid has evaporated. Transfer contents to a mixing bowl. Finely chop any large pieces of mango in the chutney. Add chutney and remaining ingredients. Blend well. Place eggplant shells in a shallow baking dish and stuff with meat mixture, mounding it high. Sprinkle generously with paprika. Place dish on rack in wok over simmering water. Cover loosely with aluminum foil. Cover wok and steam stuffed eggplant for 25 to 30 minutes. If desired, place under broiler for a few minutes to brown surface. Makes 2 large or 4 medium-size servings.

Meatballs & Green-Pepper Heroes

Perfect for after the game.

1 tablespoon oil
1 tablespoon butter
1 clove garlic, peeled, minced
2 long French-style rolls, cut in half lengthwise
1 lb. lean ground beef
1/2 cup soft bread crumbs
2 tablespoons catsup
1 teaspoon salt
1/2 teaspoon pepper
3 tablespoons flour
3 tablespoons oil, more if needed
1 large mild onion, peeled, sliced and separated into rings
1 large green pepper, seeded and cut into rings
1-1/2 cups beef broth
2 teaspoons cornstarch, dissolved in 2 tablespoons
   water
Salt and pepper to taste

Heat oil and butter in wok. Add garlic. Stir-fry for 30 seconds. Add split rolls cut-side down in a single layer. Lightly brown over medium heat until oil and butter are absorbed. Remove and set aside. Wipe wok clean with paper towel. Combine beef, bread crumbs, catsup, salt and pepper. Form into balls and roll into flour. Put 1 tablespoon of the oil in the wok. Brown 1/3 of the meatballs over medium heat. Repeat until all are browned. Set aside. Add remaining 2 tablespoons oil, onion and green pepper. Stir-fry until vegetables are soft. Return meatballs to wok, add broth. Bring to a boil. Lower heat and cover. Simmer for 15 minutes. Stir dissolved cornstarch into simmering broth. Stir until gravy thickens. Season with salt and pepper to taste. Spoon over prepared rolls. Makes 4 servings.

Veal & Lentil Pilaf

Raisins and almonds take this pilaf out of the ordinary.

1 tablespoon oil
1/3 cup slivered almonds
1/4 cup sliced onion
3/4 cup raisins
1 lb. lean ground veal
1 cup chicken broth
1-1/3 cups cold water
1 (8-oz.) pkg. lentil-pilaf mix
2 tablespoons butter

Heat oil in wok. Add almonds and onion. Stir-fry about 3 minutes until almonds are toasted and onion is tender. Add raisins and veal. Continue to stir-fry about 3 minutes. Add broth, water, pilaf mix and butter. Stir to blend. Cover, lower heat and simmer for 25 minutes or until all liquid is absorbed. Makes 6 servings.

Variation:

Substitute ground beef for ground veal.

Ground-Beef Stroganoff

Your wok makes it double-quick.

2 tablespoons oil
1/2 teaspoon salt
1/2 cup chopped shallots or green onions
1/2 cup chopped fresh mushroom caps
2 tablespoons lemon juice
1 lb. lean ground beef
1/2 cup beef broth
1 tablespoon Sauce Diable or
   1 teaspoon Worcestershire sauce with
   1 teaspoon prepared mustard
2 teaspoons cornstarch
1 cup sour cream
Salt and pepper to taste
2 or 3 cups hot cooked flat noodles
Paprika

Heat oil with salt in wok. Add shallots or green onions and mushroom caps. Stir-fry over high heat for 1 minute. Remove, sprinkle with lemon juice and set aside. Add ground beef to wok and stir-fry until no longer pink. Drain excess fat. Add broth and stir in shallots or onions and mushrooms. Mix in Sauce Diable or Worcestershire sauce with mustard. Cover and steam for 30 seconds. Lower heat. Stir cornstarch into sour cream and stir mixture into meat and vegetables. Cook, stirring until hot. Do not allow to boil after adding sour cream. Add salt and pepper to taste. Spoon over hot cooked noodles and sprinkle with paprika. Makes 4 servings.

Veal-Stuffed Zucchini

Try this Italian-style taste treat.

4 zucchini, about 6-in. long
Water
2 tablespoons oil, more if needed
1/4 cup finely chopped onion
1/2 cup cooked rice
3/4 to 1 cup Braised Veal, finely minced, page 172
1 tablespoon sauce from Braised Veal, page 172
1 egg yolk, slightly beaten
1/4 teaspoon mixed Italian herbs
3 tablespoons bread crumbs
Salt and pepper to taste
Paprika

Wash zucchini and cut in half lengthwise. Place on rack in wok over simmering water. Cover and steam for 10 minutes. Remove from wok. With a teaspoon scoop out center and chop fine. Set zucchini shells aside. Remove rack and water. Wipe wok dry and reheat. Add oil, onion and chopped zucchini. Stir-fry over low heat until tender. Add additional oil if needed. Spoon contents of wok into a mixing bowl. Add rice, veal, sauce, egg yolk, Italian herbs and 1 tablespoon of the bread crumbs. Mix thoroughly. Season lightly with salt and pepper to taste. Spoon mixture into zucchini shells and mound slightly. Cover each with remaining bread crumbs, pressing lightly into stuffing. Sprinkle with paprika. Place in shallow baking dish. Place dish on rack in wok over simmering water. Cover and steam for 20 minutes or until tender. Makes 4 servings.

Variation:

Substitute cooked ham, pork or beef for Braised Veal.

Rack of Lamb a la Orange

Tell me if you've tasted more delicious lamb.

1 (3- to 3-1/2-lb.) rack of lamb, rib bones cut off
Juice of 2 lemons
Peel of 2 lemons, coarsely chopped
2 tablespoons soy sauce
1 (6-oz.) can frozen orange-juice concentrate, thawed
2 tablespoons coarsely chopped green onions
1 tablespoon chopped fresh ginger
1 teaspoon salt
1/2 teaspoon pepper
1 large navel orange, peeled, cut in thin slices, for garnish

Place rack of lamb in a large non-metal bowl. With a sharp knife gash meat on both sides. In a small bowl combine lemon juice, lemon peel, soy sauce, orange-juice concentrate, onions, ginger, salt and pepper. Mix to blend. Pour over lamb. Cover and marinate for 8 to 12 hours or overnight; turn 2 or 3 times to distribute marinade. Remove lamb; reserve marinade. Place on rack in wok over simmering water. Cover and steam meat for 20 minutes per pound or until meat can be easily pierced with a fork. Place lamb in a shallow flame-proof dish. Trim fatty layer from top. Arrange orange slices down center; spoon marinade over surface. Place under broiler for 3 or 4 minutes to glaze. Baste once or twice while glazing. Makes 4 to 6 servings.

Stuffed Cabbage Rolls

Italian herbs and tomato sauce add pizzazz to this traditional dish.

8 large cabbage leaves, tough rib ends cut off
2 tablespoons oil
2 tablespoons minced onion
1 clove garlic, minced
3/4 lb. lean ground beef
1/4 lb. ground pork or sausage
1 teaspoon tomato paste
1 cup beef broth
1/2 cup fine dry bread crumbs
1 egg, slightly beaten
1/2 teaspoon salt
1/2 teaspoon coarse-ground black pepper
1/2 teaspoon mixed Italian herbs
1 cup Italian tomato sauce, canned

Place cabbage leaves on rack in wok over simmering water. Cover and steam for 4 to 5 minutes. Remove leaves and cool. Drain and dry wok. Add oil, onion and garlic; stir-fry over low heat until limp. Combine with beef and pork or sausage in large mixing bowl. Stir tomato paste into beef broth. Add to meat with remaining ingredients except Italian tomato sauce. Gently blend mixture. Spoon evenly onto cabbage leaves. Fold in sides and roll up completely, encasing filling. Place in a single layer, seam-side down in a baking dish just large enough to hold them tightly. Pour Italian tomato sauce over rolls. Place baking dish on rack in wok over simmering water. Cover and steam for 1 hour. Makes 4 servings.

Veal Paprikash

Something different and delicious to make with leftover veal.

1 tablespoon oil
1/4 cup chopped onion
1/4 lb. mushrooms, sliced thin
1-1/2 to 2 cups cubed Braised Veal, page 170
1 tablespoon paprika, more if desired
1/2 teaspoon salt
4 oz. egg noodles
1 cup chicken broth
1 cup sour cream room temperature

Heat oil in wok. Add onion and mushrooms. Stir-fry until tender. Add veal. Stir in paprika and salt. Place noodles on top of meat and vegetables. Pour broth over noodles. Bring to a boil. Lower heat. Cover and simmer about 15 minutes, stirring occasionally. Remove wok from heat and stir in sour cream. Return to low heat. Stir gently until steamy hot. Makes 4 to 6 servings.

Variation:

Chicken or beef may be substituted for veal.

Veal Stew

Borrowed from Normandy for a cold winter night.

3/4 lb. lean veal scallops
1/2 cup flour
1 teaspoon salt
1 tablespoon oil
1 tablespoon butter
4 to 6 large mushrooms, trimmed, sliced through stems
2 stalks celery, sliced at 45-degree angle
   in 1/2-in.-lengths
1 small onion, peeled, chopped
2 medium carrots, peeled, sliced at 45-degree angle
   in thin ovals
1 medium tomato, peeled, chopped
1 medium potato, peeled, cubed
1/2 teaspoon salt
1/4 teaspoon pepper
1/2 cup chicken broth
1/4 cup dry white wine
2 tablespoons cornstarch dissolved in 2 tablespoons
   water
1/4 cup sour cream
1/4 cup minced parsley
French bread, if desired

Using a heavy cleaver or rolling pin, pound veal between
wax paper until about 1/8-inch thick. Cut in 1-1/2-inch-
strips. Mix flour with 1 teaspoon salt. Rub into veal strips
and shake off excess. Heat wok, add oil and butter. When
sizzling add veal; stir-fry over medium heat until meat is
lightly browned. Add all vegetables, 1/2 teaspoon salt and
pepper. Stir-fry about 30 seconds. Add broth. Cover and
steam over low heat until tender, about 30 minutes.

Remove with slotted spoon to heated serving dish. Add wine to cooking liquid. Cook, stirring over low heat about 1 minute. Stir in dissolved cornstarch and cook, stirring, until liquid thickens. Remove wok from heat. Stir in sour cream and parsley. Pour over vegetables and meat. If desired, serve with crusty French bread. Makes 4 servings.

Variation:

Chicken or beef may be substituted for veal.

Curried Rice With Lamb

This lamb dish will delight curry lovers.

3 eggs
1 teaspoon curry powder
1/4 teaspoon salt
2 teaspoons water
2 tablespoons oil
2 green onions, cut in 1/2-in. pieces
3 cups cold cooked rice
1/2 cup slivered toasted almonds
1/2 cup raisins
1/2 cup slivered cooked lean lamb

Beat eggs with curry powder, salt and water. Heat oil in wok. Add green onions and stir-fry about 30 seconds. Add rice and stir-fry until heated through. Add eggs to rice and stir until eggs are almost set. Stir in almonds, raisins and lamb. Makes 4 to 6 servings.

Stir-Fry Liver & Peppers

You won't believe the flavor difference.

1 lb. calves liver, sliced 1/2-in. thick
4 tablespoons wheat or all-purpose flour
1 teaspoon salt
1/2 teaspoon coarse-ground black pepper
1 teaspoon imported Hungarian paprika
2 tablespoons oil
1 clove garlic, peeled, crushed
1 (1-in.) cube fresh ginger, peeled
3 medium green peppers, seeded and cut in
   1/2-in. strips
1 tablespoon oil, more if needed
1/2 cup water
2 tablespoons sherry
2 tablespoons soy sauce
2 teaspoons cornstarch dissolved in 1 tablespoon water
3 cups hot cooked rice

Cut liver slices in 1/2-inch strips. Combine flour, salt, pepper and paprika on wax paper. Coat liver strips in mixture. Rub mixture evenly into meat; shake off excess. Set aside. Heat 2 tablespoons oil in wok. Add garlic and ginger. Stir-fry until garlic is browned. Remove and discard garlic and ginger. Add pepper strips and stir-fry about 1 minute. Cover, and steam for 2 minutes, stirring occasionally. Stir-fry about 30 seconds or until green pepper is tender, but crisp. Remove and set aside. Add 1 tablespoon oil to wok. Stir-fry liver strips, a few at a time, until lightly browned and crisp. Add additional oil as needed. Remove liver strips and set aside. Add water, sherry and soy sauce to wok. Stir in dissolved cornstarch. Add pepper strips and browned liver. Stir-fry until liquid thickens and peppers and liver are reheated. Serve over hot cooked rice. Makes 6 servings.

Spanish Veal With Almond Sauce

Barcelona gave me the inspiration for this delicious dish.

1/4 cup blanched almonds, toasted
2 tablespoons oil
1 clove garlic
1 lb. boneless veal, about 1-in. thick, sliced thin across grain
3/4 cup chicken broth
1 teaspoon cornstarch
1/4 cup sherry
Salt and pepper to taste
1/2 cup sliced pimiento-stuffed olives
2 to 3 cups hot cooked rice or noodles

Grind almonds in blender. Set aside. Heat oil with garlic in wok. Remove browned garlic and discard. Stir-fry a few veal slices at a time over high heat. Remove when lightly browned. Add broth and return all browned meat to wok. Reduce heat. Cover and simmer for 15 minutes, stirring occasionally. Dissolve cornstarch in sherry. Add with ground almonds to wok. Cook, stirring until sauce thickens. Season with salt and pepper to taste. Stir in olives. Serve over hot cooked rice or noodles. Makes 4 to 6 servings.

Variation:

Chicken or beef may be substituted for veal.

Spanish Veal with Almond Sauce

Stir-fry Veal With Noodles

A quick "meal in one."

1 tablespoon oil
1/2 cup chopped green onion
1/2 cup diagonally sliced celery
1/2 (10-oz.) pkg. frozen peas
2 teaspoons cornstarch
1 cup sauce from Braised Veal, or canned beef gravy
1-1/2 cups thin strips Braised Veal, page 170
8 oz. cooked flat noodles
Salt and pepper to taste
Crisp fried Chinese noodles, for garnish

Heat oil in wok. Add green onion, celery and frozen peas. Stir-fry about 5 minutes. In a small bowl, blend cornstarch into sauce or gravy. Pour over stir-fried vegetables; add veal and stir until steamy hot. Add noodles. Stir and lift until well-mixed. Season with salt and pepper to taste. Cook about 30 seconds or until noodles are heated. Sprinkle with Chinese noodles. Makes 4 servings.

Curried Lamb With Snow Peas

Nine minutes cooking time and "Dinner is served."

1 (10-oz.) pkg. frozen snow peas
2 tablespoons oil
1 tablespoon curry powder, more if desired
1 lb. lean ground lamb
2 medium onions, peeled, chopped
1 teaspoon salt
1/2 teaspoon red pepper flakes, or to taste
1 (8-oz.) can tomato sauce
2 cups cooked rice

Thaw peas at room temperature for 30 minutes. Heat wok, add oil and curry powder. Stir-fry over medium heat about 30 seconds. Add lamb, onions, salt and red pepper flakes. Stir-fry about 6 to 8 minutes. Add tomato sauce and snow peas. Cover and steam until snow peas are tender. Add rice, stir until heated. Makes 4 servings.

Lamb Balls With Zucchini

Looking for a pleasantly different one-dish meal?

2 tablespoons oil
1/2 teaspoon salt
1/4 cup finely minced onion
1/4 cup finely minced celery
1 lb. lean ground lamb
1 cup soft bread crumbs

1 teaspoon Worcestershire sauce
1 egg, slightly beaten
1/4 teaspoon garlic salt
1/4 teaspoon pepper
4 tablespoons oil
2 large zucchini, about 12 oz., sliced diagonally at a
    45-degree angle in thin ovals
1 (16-oz.) can stewed tomatoes
1/2 cup beef broth
1/2 teaspoon oregano
1/2 teaspoon basil
1 teaspoon sugar
1 tablespoon cornstarch dissolved in 1/4 cup water
3 cups hot cooked noodles

Heat 2 tablespoons oil with salt in wok. Add onion and
celery. Stir-fry until soft. Spoon contents of wok over lamb
in a mixing bowl. Add bread crumbs, Worcestershire
sauce, egg, garlic salt and pepper. Mix thoroughly. Form
into 12 meatballs. Heat 2 tablespoons of the oil in wok.
Brown a few meatballs at a time over high heat. Remove
and set aside. Wipe wok clean with paper towel. Add
remaining 2 tablespoons oil to wok and heat. Add
zucchini and stir-fry about 1 minute. Return meatballs to
wok. Add tomatoes, broth, oregano, basil and sugar.
Bring to a boil. Lower heat. Cover and simmer for 20
minutes, stirring occasionally. Add dissolved cornstarch
and stir until sauce thickens. Serve over noodles. Makes 6
servings.

Pork Chops Chinese-Style

Try these flavorful chops with fewer calories.

4 pork chops about 3/4-in. thick, trimmed
1/4 cup chopped green onion
1 clove garlic, peeled, crushed
1/4 cup chili sauce
3/4 cup dry sherry
2 tablespoons soy sauce
2 teaspoons brown sugar
1/2 teaspoon salt

Place pork chops in a long shallow baking dish. Combine all remaining ingredients and pour over chops. Turn chops several times in marinade, piercing each with a fork several places so marinade will penetrate. Let stand at room temperature for 2 to 3 hours, turning chops frequently, or refrigerate 8 to 10 hours, turning chops occasionally. Bring to room temperature before cooking. Place a cake rack in a pie plate and arrange chops in a single layer. Place on rack in wok over simmering water. Cover and steam for 1 hour. Makes 2 to 4 servings.

Pork & Beans en Adobo

Exotic flavors from "ordinary" ingredients.

4 pork chops cut 1-in. thick
Water
1 tablespoon oil
1 clove garlic, peeled, minced
1 green pepper, seeded and cut in narrow strips
    lengthwise
2 medium tomatoes, chopped
2 cups canned black beans, drained; reserve 1/4
    cup liquid
Salt to taste
Coarse-ground black pepper to taste
1 firm ripe banana, cut in 1-in. chunks
1/2 cup unsweetened pineapple cubes
1/4 cup minced parsley
2 cups hot cooked rice

Place pork chops in wok and just cover with water. Simmer over medium heat until liquid evaporates. Brown chops, turning once. Remove from wok. Discard bones and slice meat in 1/2-inch-thick strips. Heat oil in wok, add garlic and green pepper. Stir-fry about 1 minute. Add tomatoes and stir-fry about 2 minutes. Cover and steam about 2 minutes. Stir in beans and bean liquid. Season lightly with salt and pepper. Add pork strips, banana chunks and pineapple cubes. Push gently down into bean mixture. Cover and steam for 2 to 3 minutes. Sprinkle with minced parsley just before serving. Makes 4 to 6 servings.

Ham & Broccoli Stir-Fry

Only ten minutes from refrigerator to table.

1 (10-oz.) pkg. frozen broccoli spears, thawed
2 tablespoons oil
1 teaspoon salt
1 clove garlic, peeled, minced
1/2 cup thinly sliced celery
1 green pepper, seeded and cut in thin strips
1/4 cup chopped onion
1 large tomato, chopped
1/4 teaspoon poultry seasoning
1 cup chopped cooked ham
2 teaspoons cornstarch dissolved in 2
    tablespoons water

Cut off broccoli flowerets and set aside. Trim and cut stalks diagonally in thin strips. Heat oil with salt in wok. Add garlic, celery, green pepper, onion and broccoli stalks. Stir-fry about 1 minute. Add tomato, poultry seasoning and ham. Cover and steam for 5 minutes, stirring occasionally. Place broccoli flowerets on top of vegetables and ham. Cover and steam for 5 minutes. Uncover and stir in dissolved cornstarch. Cook until thickened. Makes 4 servings.

Indonesian Stir-Fry

Pork and shrimp blend for a superb accent.

1 (8-oz.) pkg. flat noodles
1/4 teaspoon salt
Water
Few drops of oil
3 tablespoons oil
1/2 cup chopped green onion
1 clove garlic, peeled, minced
8 oz. raw shrimp, peeled, deveined and coarsely
   chopped
1 cup chicken broth
1 cup shredded cooked pork
2 tablespoons soy sauce
2 teaspoons cornstarch dissolved in 2 tablespoons
   water
Red-pepper flakes
1 cup Chinese fried noodles

Drop noodles into a large pot of rapidly boiling salted water. Add a few drops of oil. Boil for 5 minutes. Drain. Place in a warm bowl. Add 2 teaspoons oil and toss until evenly coated. Spread on a warm platter. Add remaining oil to wok over medium heat. Add onion and garlic. Stir-fry about 1 minute. Add shrimp. Continue to stir-fry until shrimp are firm and pink. Pour in broth and bring to a boil. Lower heat to simmer. Add pork. Stir in soy sauce and dissolved cornstarch. Cook, stirring until sauce thickens. Spoon over cooked flat noodles. Sprinkle with red-pepper flakes and Chinese fried noodles. Makes 4 to 6 servings.

Green Noodles With Ham

A quick meal-in-one.

2 tablespoons oil
1 (8-oz.) pkg. flat green noodles, cooked
2 tablespoons oil
2 tablespoons chopped green onion
1 cup slivered cooked ham
1 (6-oz.) can slivered bamboo shoots, drained
1 (2-oz.) can sliced mushrooms, undrained
1/2 cup chicken broth
2 tablespoons soy sauce
2 teaspoons cornstarch dissolved in 2 tablespoons
   water

Heat 2 tablespoons oil in wok over high heat. When almost sizzling, add noodles, tossing them with 2 wooden spoons as you would a salad. When evenly coated, transfer to a deep bowl. Add to wok 2 tablespoons oil, green onion, ham and bamboo shoots. Stir-fry about 2 minutes. Spoon mixture over noodles. Add undrained mushrooms and broth. Bring to a boil. Lower heat so liquid simmers and add soy sauce. Stir in dissolved cornstarch. Cook, stirring until sauce is slightly thickened. Return noodles and ham mixture to wok and heat thoroughly. Makes 4 to 6 servings.

Pork en Adobo With Cabbage

Something new with old favorites.

1 cup finely chopped cabbage
Boiling water
1 lb. lean fillet of pork, cut in 1/2-in.-thick slices
1 clove garlic, peeled, minced
1/4 cup cider vinegar
1 teaspoon salt
1/2 teaspoon coarse-ground black pepper
Boiling water or chicken broth
2 teaspoons sugar
Soy or steak sauce
2 cups cooked rice, noodles, or mashed potatoes

In wok, cover cabbage with boiling water. Boil over medium heat until cabbage is tender but still slightly crisp, about 10 minutes. Drain in colander and set aside. Place pork, garlic, vinegar, salt and pepper in a non-metal bowl and let stand about 10 minutes. Place in wok with enough boiling water or broth to just cover meat. Cover and simmer until liquid evaporates. Stir-fry meat until lightly browned. Add cabbage and sprinkle with sugar. Stir-fry until heated. Season lightly with soy or steak sauce. Serve over rice, noodles or mashed potatoes. Makes 4 servings.

Mango Chutney

You only need 3 or 4 mangoes for several jars of homemade chutney.

3 or 4 mangoes, or enough to make 3 cups, peeled,
   seeded and cut into 1/2-in. strips about 3 inches long
2 cups light-brown sugar, firmly packed
1-1/2 cups cider vinegar
1/2 cup lime juice
1 cup seedless raisins
1 cup peeled and chopped onion
2 large cloves garlic, peeled, minced
1/4 cup fresh peeled and chopped ginger
1 teaspoon dry mustard
1 teaspoon red-pepper flakes

Combine ingredients in a heavy saucepan. Bring to a full boil. Lower heat and simmer very gently for about 1 hour. Remove from heat and let stand until cool. Cover and refrigerate 12 hours. Reheat and bring to a full boil, lower heat and simmer for 1 hour. Repeat refrigeration and reheating once more, then ladle into clean jars and seal. Makes about four 1/2-pint jars.

Mexican-Style Macaroni & Sausage

Here's a three-way compromise—Chinese, Mexican and American—that's easy on your budget.

1/2 lb. small elbow macaroni
1/4 teaspoon salt
Water
1 teaspoon oil
2 teaspoons oil
1 lb. chorizo or spicy pork sausage
1/2 cup minced onion
1 (1-lb.) can tomato sauce
1 teaspoon crumbled oregano
Salt and pepper to taste
1 cup shredded Monterey Jack or mild Cheddar Cheese

Drop macaroni in a large pot of boiling salted water. Add 1 teaspoon oil and cook until tender. Drain. Transfer to a heated bowl. Add 2 teaspoons oil and toss until macaroni is coated. Remove sausage skin. Heat wok and add sausage. Break sausage apart and stir-fry until well browned. Add onion and stir-fry until limp. Stir in tomato sauce and oregano. Cook, stirring occasionally, until bubbly hot. Season with salt and pepper. Add macaroni and cook, stirring until heated. Stir in cheese; blend quickly. Cheese need not melt completely. Serve at once. Makes 6 servings.

Spinach & Ham Stir-Fry

Walnuts make this spinach dish a crunchy treat.

2 tablespoons oil
1/4 teaspoon salt
1/2 cup coarsely chopped walnuts
1 cup slivered cooked ham
1 lb. spinach, washed, stems removed
1 tablespoon soy sauce

Heat oil with salt in wok. Add walnuts and ham. Stir-fry about 1 minute. Add spinach. Cover and steam for 1 minute. Uncover, add soy sauce. Stir-fry until spinach is still slightly crisp. Makes 6 servings.

Indonesian Pork Curry

Give leftovers an exotic taste.

2 tablespoons sherry
1/2 cup raisins
2 tablespoons oil
1/2 cup chopped onion
2 teaspoons curry powder
1 (8-oz.) pkg. chicken-flavored rice with vermicelli
2-1/2 cups water
1 to 1-1/2 cups shredded cooked pork
1/2 cup slivered almonds

Pour sherry over raisins and let stand. Heat oil in wok. Add onion and stir-fry about 1 minute. Stir in curry powder and rice with vermicelli. Stir-fry about 30 seconds. Add water and stir to blend. Cover and simmer for 25 minutes or until water has been absorbed by rice. Uncover and stir occasionally. Stir in raisins, pork and almonds. Serve very hot. Makes 4 to 6 servings.

Pork & Cabbage With Noodles

A one-dish dinner that's simply great.

2 tablespoons oil
1/2 lb. boneless smoked pork chops, cut in narrow strips
3 cups shredded cabbage
1 cup water
1 cup chicken broth
4 oz. fine noodles
1/2 teaspoon salt
1/4 teaspoon pepper

Heat oil in wok. Add pork strips and stir-fry about 3 minutes. Stir in cabbage, continuing to stir-fry about 3 minutes. Add water and broth. Bring to a full boil. Stir in noodles, salt and pepper. Cover and steam for 10 minutes or until most liquid has been absorbed by noodles. Stir occasionally. Makes 4 servings.

Chinese Fruited Pork

Your friends will rave about this unusual and different dish.

6 loin chops, cut 1/2-in. thick
2 tablespoons soy sauce
1 teaspoon sesame oil
1/4 teaspoon pepper
1 tablespoon cornstarch
3/4 cup oil
1 tablespoon oil
1 (10-oz.) pkg. frozen snow peas, partially thawed
1/4 cup water
1 (1-lb.) can apricot halves, drained; reserve
    1/4 cup syrup
1 teaspoon cornstarch
3 cups hot cooked rice

Trim bones and fat from chops. Place meat between wax paper and pound with a mallet to 1/4-inch thickness. Cut into 1″ x 1/2″ cubes and place in a bowl. Add soy sauce, sesame oil, pepper and cornstarch. Blend to coat meat. Let stand 15 minutes. Heat 3/4 cup oil in wok over high heat. Add pork cubes and cook, stirring, about 3 to 4 minutes. Remove and set aside. Drain and wipe wok with paper towel. Add 1 tablespoon oil and heat. Add snow peas and stir-fry about 30 seconds. Add water, cover and steam about 30 seconds. Add apricots and pork. Stir-fry about 30 seconds. Dissolve cornstarch in reserved apricot syrup. Add to wok and stir until sauce thickens. Serve over hot cooked rice. Makes 6 servings.

Pork With Chinese Vegetables

Colorful pork-vegetable combo.

3 tablespoons sherry
1-1/2 to 2 cups thin strips cooked pork
2 tablespoons catsup
2 tablespoons soy sauce
1 teaspoon brown sugar
2 teaspoons cornstarch dissolved in 2 tablespoons
  water
1 cup chicken broth
2 tablespoons oil
1 medium onion, peeled, chopped
1 (about 1-lb.) can Chinese vegetables, well-drained
1 cup shredded lettuce, packed down
2 to 3 cups cooked rice
Chinese fried noodles, if desired

Sprinkle sherry over pork strips. Let stand about 30
minutes. In a saucepan, stir catsup, soy sauce, brown
sugar and dissolved cornstarch in broth. Stir over low heat
until sauce is smooth. Set aside. Heat oil in wok. Add onion
and stir-fry about 1 minute. Drain sherry from pork into
sauce. Add pork to wok. Stir-fry about 30 seconds. Add
Chinese vegetables. Stir until heated. Stir in sauce, top with
shredded lettuce. Cover and steam for 30 seconds. Stir to
blend. Serve over hot cooked rice. If desired, sprinkle each
serving with Chinese fried noodles. Makes 4 to 6 servings.

Sweet & Sour Pork

A traditional favorite demonstrates your wok talents.

1 lb. lean pork, cut in 1-in. cubes.
Water
2 tablespoons soy sauce
1 cup flour
1 egg, slightly beaten with 1 tablespoon water
Oil for deep frying
1 tablespoon oil
1/2 teaspoon salt
1 clove garlic, peeled, crushed
1 green pepper, seeded, cut in 1-in. squares
1 carrot, peeled, sliced at a 45-degree angle in thin ovals
1/2 cup water
Sweet & Sour Sauce, see below
1 (8-oz.) can unsweetened pineapple chunks, drained;
   reserve 1/2 cup juice
2 cups cooked white rice

Sweet & Sour Sauce:

3/4 cup vinegar
3/4 cup sugar
1/2 cup reserved unsweetened pineapple juice
   (from canned pineapple)
1/2 cup water
1 tablespoon catsup
2 tablespoons soy sauce
1 tablespoon cornstarch
1/4 cup sherry

Place pork cubes in a saucepan. Cover with water. Bring to
a boil and reduce heat. Simmer for 20 minutes or until no

longer pink in center. Drain. Cool to room temperature. Toss cubes with soy sauce. Roll each in flour, then in beaten egg and again in flour. Place on a rack and let stand for 5 to 10 minutes. Fill wok with oil to center depth of 2 inches. Heat to 375°F (191°C). Fry pork cubes in hot oil, a few at a time, until lightly browned and crisp. Drain and set aside. Pour oil from wok. Wipe clean with paper towel. Heat 1 tablespoon oil with salt in wok. Add garlic and stir against sides until browned; remove and discard garlic. Add green pepper and carrot. Stir-fry about 1 minute. Pour in water. Cover and steam about 3 minutes or until crisp-tender. Stir-fry until liquid has evaporated. Pour in Sweet & Sour Sauce. Add pork and pineapple. Stir gently until meat is reheated. Serve over hot cooked rice. Makes 4 servings.

Sweet & Sour Sauce:

In a small non-metal pan, combine vinegar, sugar, reserved pineapple juice, water and catsup. Stir over low heat until sugar dissolves. Add soy sauce. Dissolve cornstarch in sherry. Stir into sauce. Stir over low heat until thickened.

Curried Pork With Noodles

Make this dish your own pork "special."

1 (8-oz.) pkg. fine noodles
1/4 teaspoon salt
Water
Few drops of oil
2 teaspoons oil
1 small purple onion, peeled, sliced
1 to 2 cups water
1/2 cup catsup
1 teaspoon Worcestershire sauce
1/2 teaspoon salt
1/2 teaspoon sugar
1 tablespoon curry powder
1/2 cup chicken or beef broth
1 cup shredded cooked pork
1 tomato, cut in wedges

Drop noodles into a large pot of rapidly boiling salted water. Add a few drops of oil. Cook until noodles rise to the surface and are pliable, about 1 minute. Drain. Place on a large platter and toss with a little oil. Cover onion slices with water and boil for 2 to 3 minutes. Drain, blot dry. Cut onion slices in half. In a small bowl, combine catsup, Worcestershire sauce, 1/2 teaspoon salt and sugar. Set aside. Place wok over low heat. Add curry powder and stir constantly until curry is slightly browned and pungent. Pour in broth and stir to blend. Turn heat to high. Add onion slices, and shredded pork. Bring to a boil. Stir in catsup mixture. Add tomato wedges. Stir until heated. Spoon over noodles. Makes 4 servings.

Philippine Pineapple Pork en Adobo

You'll love the exotic flavor of this dish.

1 medium green pepper, seeded, cut in strips lengthwise
4 to 6 green onions, trimmed, cut in 1/2-in. pieces
Boiling water
1 lb. lean fillet of pork cut in 1/2-in.-thick slices
1/3 cup unsweetened pineapple juice
3/4 cup chicken broth
Salt and pepper to taste
Soy or steak sauce
Cooked rice, noodles or split toasted hero buns

Put green-pepper strips and green onions in boiling water in wok. Boil over medium heat for 2 minutes. Drain in a colander. Set aside. Place pork, pineapple juice and broth in wok. Bring to a boil. Cover, lower heat and simmer for 10 minutes. Uncover. With a wet paper towel wipe inside of wok where liquid has left a sticky glaze. If left on wok, it may cause a burned taste. Continue to cook, stirring until most of the liquid has evaporated. Add green pepper and onions. Stir-fry about 2 to 3 minutes. Season with salt and pepper to taste, and soy or steak sauce. Serve over rice, noodles, or split and toasted hero buns. Makes 4 servings.

Variation:

Substitute chicken, beef, veal or lamb for pork.

So-Good Spareribs

Try these and you'll never want any other kind.

1-1/2 lbs. trimmed spareribs
1/2 cup brown sugar, firmly packed
2 tablespoons cider vinegar
1/4 cup catsup
1 teaspoon dry mustard
1 teaspoon Worcestershire sauce
1 teaspoon prepared horseradish
2 teaspoons cornstarch dissolved in 2 tablespoons
    water, if desired

Place trimmed spareribs on a rack in wok over simmering water. Cover and steam for 45 minutes or until tender. Place in a long baking dish. Combine remaining ingredients and pour over ribs. Place dish on rack in wok over simmering water. Cover and steam for 30 minutes. While steaming, uncover wok and turn spareribs in sauce several times. Remove ribs to serving platter. If desired, thicken sauce with dissolved cornstarch. Spoon over ribs and serve hot. Makes 4 servings.

Pork With Chinese Cabbage

Your family will ask you to fix this more often.

2 tablespoons oil
1/2 teaspoon salt
1 carrot, peeled, cut in 1-in.-long "matchsticks"
1 cup diagonally sliced celery
1 small zucchini, trimmed, cut in 1-in.-long
   "matchsticks"
1/2 cup water
1-1/2 to 2 cups boned and cubed cooked pork, see
   Chinese Pork in Plum Sauce, page 37
1/2 cup frozen snow peas
2 cups shredded Chinese cabbage
1 teaspoon sugar
2 teaspoons cornstarch, dissolved
1/4 cup soy sauce
2 or 3 cups hot cooked rice

Heat oil with salt in wok. Add carrot strips, celery and zucchini strips. Stir-fry about 1 minute. Add 1/4 cup of the water. Cover and steam for 1 minute. Uncover, add remaining water. Stir-fry about 1 minute and steam for 1 more minute until vegetables are cooked but slightly crisp. Add pork cubes and stir-fry about 30 seconds. Add snow peas and cabbage. Sprinkle with sugar. Stir cabbage and peas into pork and other vegetables. Cover and steam for 30 seconds or until cabbage is crisp-tender. Dissolve cornstarch in soy sauce. Stir into pork and vegetables. Serve over rice. Makes 4 to 6 servings.

Note:

Chinese cabbage, sometimes known as *long cabbage*, is now found in many supermarkets. It is a cylinder of close-fitted crinkly leaves a foot or more long and about 6 inches in diameter. More delicate than plain cabbage and heartier than lettuce, it's perfect for stir-frying.

Noodles & Sausage Napoli

Add green salad and crusty bread for a Neopolitan feast.

2 tablespoons oil
1 lb. sweet Italian sausage, sliced
1/2 cup chopped onion
1 clove garlic, peeled, minced
1 (8-oz.) pkg. fine noodles
2 (1-lb.) cans Italian-style tomatoes with basil
1/2 cup water
1/2 teaspoon mixed Italian herbs
1 teaspoon salt
1/2 cup grated Parmesan cheese
1/2 cup minced parsley

Heat oil in wok. Add sausage slices and brown on both sides. Remove sausage and set aside. Add onions and garlic. Stir-fry about 1 minute and push to sides of wok. Add noodles and stir-fry until golden. Pour in tomatoes and water; return sausage to wok. Season with Italian herbs and salt. Cover and simmer about 10 minutes; stir occasionally, chopping and breaking up tomatoes. When noodles are tender, stir in cheese. Sprinkle with parsley and serve at once. Makes 4 to 6 servings.

Ham With Vegetables

Use leftover ham for this superb supper dish!

2 tablespoons oil
1/2 teaspoon salt
1 medium red onion, peeled, chopped
1-1/2 to 2 cups slivered cooked ham, see
  Braised Ham, page 227
1 cup cooked green beans
1 cup cooked red kidney beans
6 to 8 water chestnuts, drained, chopped
1/4 teaspoon coarse-ground black pepper
1 teaspoon sugar
1 tablespoon cider vinegar
2 tablespoons chili sauce
2 teaspoons cornstarch
1/4 cup chicken broth or water
12 cherry tomatoes

Heat oil with salt in wok. Add onion and stir-fry until soft. Add ham and stir-fry about 30 seconds. Add beans and water chestnuts. Season with pepper and sugar. Add vinegar and chili sauce. Dissolve cornstarch in broth or water. Add to wok. Stir until liquid thickens. Add tomatoes. Stir about 30 seconds, until mixture is heated. Makes 6 servings.

Wisconsin-Style Pork & Vegetables

See what frozen vegetables and a little imagination can do.

2 tablespoons oil
1/2 teaspoon salt
6 oz. smoked boned pork chops, cut in narrow strips
1/2 cup chopped onion
1/2 cup diagonally sliced celery
1 small white turnip, peeled, thinly sliced, slices
   quartered
1 small tart apple, peeled, seeded and coarsely chopped
1/4 cup chicken broth
1 teaspoon Worcestershire sauce
1 (10-oz.) pkg. frozen Wisconsin-style mixed
   vegetables with seasoning mix, partially thawed
1 teaspoon cornstarch dissolved in 2 tablespoons water
2 cups hot cooked noodles

Heat oil with salt in wok. Add pork strips, onion, celery, turnip and apple. Stir-fry about 1 minute. Add broth and Worcestershire sauce. Bring to a full boil. Add partially thawed frozen vegetables; reserve package of seasoning mix. Cover and steam about 4 minutes. Add dissolved cornstarch and stir until liquid thickens. Serve over hot cooked noodles. Sprinkle with package of seasoning mix from frozen vegetables. Makes 4 servings.

Millionaire's Hot Dogs

Tart and bubbly.

1 (1-lb.) can sauerkraut
2 small very-tart apples, peeled, cored and finely chopped
1 cup champagne
8 frankfurters
8 small new potatoes
2 teaspoons cornstarch dissolved in 2 tablespoons
  champagne

Place sauerkraut in a colander and rinse well under cold running water. Drain and blot dry with paper towel. Place in a long shallow glass baking dish. Add chopped apples. Pour in champagne. Place frankfurters on top. Place dish on rack in wok over simmering water. Arrange potatoes around dish on the same rack. Cover and steam for 30 minutes. Uncover, remove frankfurters and potatoes. Stir dissolved cornstarch into sauerkraut and stir until liquid has thickened. Arrange sauerkraut on a long platter. Top with frankfurters and surround with potatoes. Makes 4 servings.

Variation:

Substitute apple cider for champagne.

How To Make
Millionaire's Hot Dogs

Place hot dogs on top of sauerkraut-apple mixture. Set the baking dish on a rack in the wok over simmering water. Arrange the potatoes on the rack around the dish.

Place sauerkraut on a platter. Arrange the hot dogs on top and the potatoes on the side.

Pork Fried Rice

Great party fare with Chinese egg rolls, preserved kumquats and fresh pineapple cubes.

3 tablespoons oil, more if needed
2 or 3 drops sesame oil, if desired
1/2 cup chopped green onion
1 clove garlic, peeled, minced
4 cups cooked rice, chilled
1/2 cup chopped water chestnuts
1 cup cooked pork, shredded
2 tablespoons soy sauce
Coarse-ground black pepper
   to taste
3 eggs, slightly beaten
1/2 cup bean sprouts
Soy sauce

Heat oil in wok. Add sesame oil, if desired. Add green onions and garlic. Stir-fry over moderate heat until limp. Add rice. With a spatula or large wooden spoon, stir until the grains are thoroughly coated with oil and begin to color lightly, about 7 to 8 minutes. Add a little additional oil if rice seems dry. Mix in water chestnuts and pork. Stir-fry about 3 to 4 minutes. Stir in soy sauce and season lightly with pepper. Pour eggs over rice. Stir and lift for about 1 minute until eggs are cooked. Stir in bean sprouts and serve. Pass additional soy sauce at the table. Makes 4 to 6 servings.

Absolutely Superb Pork Chow Mein

Best-tasting Chinese dish this side of China.

1 (8-oz.) pkg. fine noodles
1/4 teaspoon salt
Water
Few drops of oil
1/4 cup oil
2 tablespoons oil
1/4 lb. fresh mushrooms, thinly sliced through stems
1/4 cup minced green onions
4 cooked pork chops, boned, fat removed and sliced
   in thin strips, see Pork Chops Chinese-Style, page 201
1/2 lb. raw shrimp, peeled, deveined and coarsely
   chopped
1 cup chopped spinach leaves, stems removed
1 tablespoon soy sauce
1 tablespoon sherry
2 teaspoons cornstarch dissolved in 1/2 cup chicken
   broth

Drop noodles into a large pot of rapidly boiling, salted water. Add a few drops of oil. Cook until noodles rise to the surface and are pliable, about 1 minute. Drain. Place in a large bowl and toss with 1/4 cup oil. Heat wok, add noodles. Stir-fry until a few noodles are lightly browned. Remove, spread on a warm serving platter. Heat 2 tablespoons of oil in wok. Add mushrooms and green onions. Stir-fry over high heat about 1 minute. Add pork strips and shrimp. Stir-fry until shrimp are firm and pink. Add spinach and stir-fry about 30 seconds. Add soy sauce and sherry. Cover and steam for 30 seconds. Pour in cornstarch mixture. Stir until slightly thickened. Spoon over noodles. Makes 6 servings.

Beef Broth

A real time and money saver.

3 lbs. shank of beef, bone-in
1 veal knuckle bone, if available
Water
1 large onion, peeled, quartered
3 carrots, peeled and cut in chunks
2 cloves garlic, split
3 or 4 celery stalks with leaves
Several sprigs parsley
1 teaspoon salt
1/2 cup dry red wine

Preheat oven to 400°F (204°C). Place meat and bones in large pan and roast in preheated oven for 15 to 20 minutes or until brown. Place contents in a large pot, cover with water. Add onion, carrots, garlic, celery, parsley, salt and wine. Bring to a boil, then lower heat to simmer. Cook uncovered for 4 to 5 hours. Let cool. Remove meat from bones and discard bones. Strain broth into a large bowl; discard vegetables. Refrigerate broth until fat rises to the surface and congeals. Remove and discard fat. Transfer broth to freezer containers, cover tightly and freeze until needed. Makes 3 to 4 pints broth.

Braised Ham

My favorite way to cook ham.

2 tablespoons oil
4 tablespoons coarsely chopped green onion
1 (4- to 5-lb.) ham, butt end, bone-in
1/2 cup water
1 cup brown sugar, firmly packed
2 tablespoons mustard
1 tablespoon flour

Heat oil in wok. Add onion and stir-fry until soft. Place ham on top of onions, add water. Lower heat to medium. Cover and braise ham for 15 minutes per pound. Uncover. Remove rind and excess fat. Score remaining fat in a diamond design. Mix brown sugar with mustard and flour to a smooth paste. Spread over scored fat. Cover and continue to cook ham for 5 to 10 minutes or until glaze melts. Place ham on a platter. Let stand 15 to 20 minutes before carving. Makes 8 to 10 servings.

DESSERTS

Desserts from a Chinese wok? I didn't believe it until I tried it—but what desserts! I never made more perfect puddings, more moist and delicate cakes or such golden-crisp, flaky deep-fried pies. And testing these deep-fried pies led to a marvelous brand-new recipe, Deep-Fried Eclairs, page 237.

But why a wok? Certainly all these desserts can be cooked in conventional pots and pans, but cakes won't be as moist, puddings won't be as even-textured and light, custard will be less delicate and fried pastries not so crisp. Furthermore, in conventional pots and pans, they all take longer to cook and cost considerably more in fuel. The amount of electricity to steam a cake in a wok is only a fraction of that consumed by an electric oven for the same amount of time. Deep-frying, too, is less expensive with a wok. You need far less oil than with a conventional deep fryer and that's no small consideration. The reason a wok is economical in time and money is its shape. Steamed desserts are surrounded by intense, moist, even heat. Deep-fried foods form a crisp coating the instant they are dropped into the hot oil because the wok's shape allows oil to reach high temperatures without burning or smoking.

I think the perfect ending to a meal is a great homemade dessert with a fragrant cup of coffee. It's important to balance the dessert with the rest of the meal. A light main course calls for a substantial sweet and vice versa. I've included a few menu suggestions in the front of each recipe section to help you plan delicious, well-balanced meals.

Steamed Puddings

Steamed puddings are my favorite desserts. Festive enough for the most elegant dinner party but 1—2—3 easy to make in a wok. Steamed puddings are lighter in calories than cakes and less expensive than pies or cakes. Plus, they are a lot less trouble to make. If you are concerned about cholesterol, steamed puddings with their low-fat content taste as sinfully rich as any dessert, without the risks of fat-laden pastry. The real reason for adding steamed puddings to your repertoire is because they taste so wonderfully good. Served plain or sauced with a flair, they are a favorite answer to "What's for dessert?"

All of the puddings here call for a 6-cup ring mold but they can be made in other 6-cup shapes. I believe you will prefer the ring type because it fits comfortably in your wok and is decorative when unmolded. For special occasions, fill the center with ice cream or sweetened whipped cream—try folding a quarter of a cup of chopped candied orange peel into the whipped cream.

Cakes

There is no way you can have the fresh delicate taste of a homemade cake unless it is in fact homemade. I regard cake making as a highly pleasurable hobby, but I never dreamed of steaming cakes in a wok. When I began researching this book a very knowledgeable Chinese restaurateur asked me if I planned to include Chinese steamed sponge cake. I'd never even heard of it. He gave me the recipe and I politely thanked him and filed it away with all the other scraps in my hand bag. I don't know why I decided to try it. I was astonished by the results: a feather-light moist sponge cake better than any other sponge cake I had ever made. Emboldened by this success, I tried my own favorite recipe for butter cake, a heavy pound cake I've made for years. To say it was a success is putting it mildly. It had a velvety moistness I'd never achieved in a conventional oven. I believe almost any cake can be steamed to advantage in a wok.

Space only allows room for a limited number of cakes here, but these I absolutely guarantee. They have been tested and retested by me, my sister, and Elsie. You can be sure of perfection.

If you embark on cakes as a hobby, here are a few tips I have learned over 25 years of happy cake making:

Butter must be very soft before you start to cream it with the sugar.

Cream butter and sugar by hand or with a rotary mixer until very light and fluffy and no trace of "grittiness" remains.

Eggs separate more easily when cold, but let them stand at room temperature for at least one hour before beating. Eggs beat to a much greater volume when they are almost warm. This is why a French chef uses only a copper bowl for beating egg whites. Heat generated by the metal beater against the copper increases the volume of the egg whites.

Beat egg whites with a French wire whisk. Rotary beaters do not do the best job because they do not create sufficient air volume to get the whites as puffy as you want them.

When the recipe calls for well-beaten egg yolks, *really* beat them. They should be thick and lemon-colored.

If the recipe calls for cake flour, never substitute regular flour.

I like to butter my cake pans generously, then dust with granulated sugar. This assures a perfect "turn out" every time.

INFORMAL DINNER PARTY

Boston Beef & Noodles, page 148
Mocha-Nut Pudding, page 254

DINNER WITH A SENSE OF HUMOR

Popcorn With Champagne
Millionaire's Hot Dogs, page 224
Brandied Apple Pudding, page 261

EAST MEETS WEST

East-West Stir-Fry, page 175
Rice
Orange-Lemon Pudding, page 247

BARBECUE SPECIAL

So-Good Spareribs, page 219
Steamed Sweet Potatoes
Purple Onion & Orange Salad
Pineapple Flan, page 250

Down-East Indian Pudding

A New England classic.

Butter for mold
1/4 cup yellow cornmeal
1/4 cup cold milk
2 cups scalded milk
4 tablespoons butter, room temperature
1/2 cup dark molasses
1 teaspoon salt
1 teaspoon cinnamon
Heavy cream, if desired

Generously butter a 1-quart mold. In a large mixing bowl, stir cornmeal into cold milk; blend until smooth. Add scalded milk and butter. Stir until butter has melted. Stir in molasses, salt and cinnamon. Pour into prepared mold. Place on rack in wok over simmering water. Cover wok and steam for 2 hours or until firm. Check at the end of the first hour and add hot water to wok as needed. Serve warm or cold with heavy cream, if desired. Makes 6 servings.

Baba au Rhum

Baba is the French word for a cake made with yeast. This one is steeped in rum.

Butter for ring mold
Sugar for ring mold
1 envelope active dry yeast

1/2 cup lukewarm water
1/4 cup lukewarm milk
2 cups flour
4 eggs, slightly beaten, room temperature
1/2 teaspoon salt
1 tablespoon sugar
1/2 cup very soft butter
1/2 cup dark rum
1/2 cup brown sugar, firmly packed
1/2 cup dark rum

Generously butter a 6-cup ring mold. Sprinkle with sugar, rotating mold to distribute sugar evenly. Dissolve yeast in lukewarm water; let soften for 5 minutes. Add lukewarm milk and stir well. Place the flour in a large mixing bowl, make a well in the center and add eggs. Beat thoroughly. Add yeast mixture, salt and sugar. Beat well with a wooden spoon until dough is soft and sticky to the touch. Cover with a towel and let rise in a warm place until double in bulk. Punch down and spread surface of dough with soft butter; work butter into dough. Spoon dough evenly into mold. Mold should be no more than 2/3 full. Again, cover and let rise in a warm place until double in bulk. Place mold on rack in wok over simmering water. Cover wok and steam for 45 to 50 minutes or until Baba tests done with a toothpick. Invert Baba onto a cake rack and cool. Combine 1/2 cup of rum and brown sugar. Stir until sugar dissolves. Return Baba to mold and pour rum syrup over Baba surface. Let stand at room temperature for 2 to 3 hours before serving. When ready to serve, transfer to serving dish. Heat remaining 1/2 cup rum and pour over surface. Ignite and bring flaming to the table. Makes 6 to 8 servings.

Mincemeat Pudding

The traditional Christmas pudding, but this one is easier and simpler for the cook.

Butter for ring mold
Sugar for ring mold
2 tablespoons butter, softened
1/2 cup brown sugar, firmly packed
1 egg
1-1/4 cups flour
2 teaspoons baking powder
2 tablespoons fine dry bread crumbs
1 cup prepared mincemeat
1/3 cup rum or brandy extract
1/2 cup chopped walnuts
Hard Sauce Stars, see below

Hard Sauce Stars:

1/2 cup butter, softened
1 cup powdered sugar
3 tablespoons brandy or rum extract

Generously butter a 6-cup ring mold, sprinkle with sugar. Rotate to distribute sugar evenly over bottom and sides of mold. In a large mixing bowl, cream butter and brown sugar until light and smooth. Add egg and beat to blend. Sift flour with baking powder; combine with bread crumbs. Mix mincemeat with rum or brandy extract. Alternately add flour mixture and mincemeat to batter. Blend well after each addition. Fold in walnuts. Pour into prepared mold. Place on rack in wok over simmering water. Cover wok and steam for 45 minutes. Invert to unmold. Serve warm or at room temperature with Hard Sauce Stars. Makes 6 servings.

Hard Sauce Stars:

In a small bowl, cream butter and powdered sugar together until light and fluffy. Stir in brandy or rum extract. Chill until firm enough to handle. Pat out on pastry board about 1/2-inch thick. Cut into small star shapes. Place in a single layer on aluminum foil and freeze. When frozen, pack in plastic bag and seal. Keep frozen until ready to decorate pudding.

Deep-Fried Eclairs

Crisp delicate pastry with an irresistible creme filling.

3 frozen patty shells, thawed but still cold
Oil for deep-frying
Creme Filling, see below
Powdered sugar

Creme Filling:

1 (3-5/8-oz.) pkg. vanilla-pudding mix
1-1/2 cups milk
4 tablespoons sour cream
2 tablespoons brandy or 1 teaspoon brandy extract

On a floured board, roll out pastry shells to a rectangle approximately 8" x 5". Trim edges evenly with a sharp knife. Cut each rectangle in half. Each piece should be approximately 8" x 2-1/2". Pour oil in wok to a 3-inch center depth. Heat to 375°F (191°C). Drop cold pastry strips into hot oil 2 or 3 at a time and fry until puffed and golden on both sides. Remove; drain on paper towels. When all 6 strips are fried, slit each in half horizontally. They will have puffed considerably and be hollow inside. Place in a single layer on a paper-towel-lined shallow dish. Cover with paper towels and place in a dry place until ready to assemble. To assemble, spoon chilled Creme Filling on bottom half of each eclair and cover with top half. Dust with powdered sugar and refrigerate until ready to serve. Filled puffs should be served within 2 to 3 hours to prevent pastry from losing its crispness. Makes 6 eclairs.

Creme Filling:

In a large saucepan, combine pudding mix with milk over low heat. Cook, stirring until mixture boils and begins to thicken. Remove from heat and cool to lukewarm. Stir in sour cream and brandy or brandy extract. Cover with plastic wrap to prevent a film from forming. Chill until very thick, at least 2 to 3 hours.

How To Make
Deep-Fried Eclairs

Roll out pastry shells to an 8" x 5" rectangle. Use a sharp knife to trim the edges and cut in half. Work quickly because pastry strips should be cold for deep-frying.

Deep-fry pastry strips, a few at a time, until they are puffed and golden.

After draining pastries on paper towels, slit each one in half horizontally. When you are ready to assemble eclairs, spoon chilled Creme Filling on each bottom half and cover with the top half. Sprinkle with powdered sugar and refrigerate.

Apricots Imperatrice

A beautiful dessert that tastes as fabulous as it looks.

Butter for ring mold
Sugar for ring mold
1 cup long-grain rice, not instant or precooked
Water
2-1/2 cups milk
1/3 cup sugar
1 teaspoon almond extract
1 tablespoon butter
3 tablespoons sour cream
2 whole eggs, slightly beaten
3 egg yolks, slightly beaten
1 cup apricot jam
2 tablespoons kirsch liqueur
1 tablespoon water
1 (1-lb.) can apricot halves, drained
Whipped cream, if desired

Generously butter a 6-cup ring mold. Sprinkle mold with sugar; rotate to distribute evenly. Place rice in a pot with a close-fitting lid. Cover rice with water and bring to a boil. Cover and cook for 5 minutes. Remove from heat and let stand, covered, for an additional 5 minutes. Drain rice in a colander and rinse with cold water. Pour 2-1/2 cups milk into a medium-size saucepan and scald. Lower heat, add rice and cover. Cook over very low heat for 30 to 35 minutes or until all liquid has been absorbed and rice is tender. Transfer to a large mixing bowl. Stir in sugar, almond extract, butter and sour cream. Cool to lukewarm, stir in beaten eggs and yolks. In a large saucepan combine apricot jam, kirsch liqueur, water and 1/2 of the drained apricots; reserve remaining apricots. Cook mixture over medium heat until jam becomes liquid and apricots are soft enough to mash. Add 1/2 of this mixture to rice; stir to blend. Cool in refrigerator. Pack chilled rice mixture into prepared mold and place on rack in wok over simmering water. Cover wok and steam for 45 minutes or until rice is firm. Invert to unmold onto serving plate. Arrange reserved apricots in a circle on top. Refrigerate until well chilled. Press remaining apricot mixture through a sieve into a bowl. Return to a saucepan and cook, stirring over medium heat until it becomes a thick glaze. Remove from heat and refrigerate until chilled. When cold, spoon glaze over chilled rice mold and refrigerate until ready to serve. The center may be filled with sweetened whipped cream if desired. Makes 6 to 8 servings.

Orange-Pineapple Bundt Cake

A beautiful cake with a lovely fresh flavor.

Butter for bundt pan
Sugar for bundt pan
1/2 cup butter, softened
1 cup sugar
4 eggs
2 cups flour
2 teaspoons baking powder
1 tablespoon grated orange peel
1/2 cup orange juice
Pineapple Sauce, see below

Pineapple Sauce:

1/2 cup sugar
2 tablespoons cornstarch
1 cup (8-1/4-oz. can) crushed pineapple in heavy syrup, drained; reserve syrup
1/2 cup orange juice

Generously butter a 3-quart bundt pan. Sprinkle with sugar, rotating pan to distribute sugar evenly on sides and bottom. In a large mixing bowl, cream butter and sugar until light and fluffy. Add eggs one at a time, beating well after each addition. Sift flour and baking powder together and set aside. Combine orange peel and orange juice. Alternately add flour mixture and orange juice to batter. Beat well after each addition. Pour into prepared pan. Place on rack in wok over simmering water. Cover wok and steam for 1 hour or until knife inserted in center comes out clean. Remove from wok, invert onto serving plate. Cool. Spoon Pineapple Sauce over entire cake. Makes 10 servings.

Pineapple Sauce:

While cake is cooking, combine sugar and cornstarch in a small saucepan. Add reserved pineapple syrup and orange juice. Stir until smooth. Heat to boiling, stirring constantly, until thickened. Add crushed pineapple and stir to blend. Spoon over cooled cake.

Bananas Flambé

A superb encore for an elegant dinner.

4 large ripe bananas, peeled, cut in half lengthwise,
   each piece cut in half
1/2 cup sugar
1/4 cup slivered almonds
1/2 cup brandy or kirsch liqueur

Place banana pieces in shallow baking dish; sprinkle with sugar, then with almonds. Pour 1/4 cup of the brandy or kirsch liqueur over bananas. Place on rack in wok over simmering water. Cover wok. Steam for 10 to 15 minutes or until bananas are tender. Remove from wok. Place remaining 1/4 cup brandy or kirsch liqueur in custard cup on rack in wok. Cover and allow liqueur to heat until just warm, about 4 or 5 minutes. Pour over hot bananas and ignite. After flames die out, spoon bananas and liqueur onto serving plates. Makes 4 servings.

Applesauce Bundt Cake

*This rich, moist cake keeps well—in a good
hiding place.*

Butter for bundt pan
Sugar for bundt pan
1/2 cup butter, softened
1 cup brown sugar, firmly packed
1/2 cup granulated sugar

2 eggs
2 cups flour
1 teaspoon baking soda
1/2 teaspoon salt
1 tablespoon cinnamon
1 teaspoon nutmeg
1 (16-oz.) can applesauce
3/4 cup chopped pitted dates
3/4 cup seedless raisins
1/2 cup chopped black walnuts

Generously butter a 3-quart bundt pan. Sprinkle with sugar, rotating to coat sides and bottom evenly. In a large mixing bowl, cream butter, brown sugar and granulated sugar until light and fluffy. Add eggs one at a time, beating well after each addition. Sift flour, baking soda, salt, cinnamon and nutmeg together. Set aside. Alternately add applesauce and flour mixture to batter. Blend well. Stir in dates, raisins and walnuts. Stir to blend. Spoon into prepared pan. Place on rack in wok over simmering water. Cover wok and steam for 1 hour. Uncover and add additional hot water as needed, cover and continue steaming for 45 minutes more or until knife inserted in center comes out clean. Remove from wok. Invert to unmold onto serving plate. Serve warm or cold. Makes 10 to 12 servings.

Variation:

Sprinkle cake generously with brandy and wrap in a cloth napkin. Store in a tight container for a week before slicing.

Applesauce Bundt Cake

onge Cake

Delicately light and moist.

Oil for ring mold
Sugar for ring mold
5 eggs, room temperature
1 cup cake flour
1 teaspoon baking powder
1 cup sugar
1/2 teaspoon vanilla, almond or lemon extract
Powdered sugar

Place rack over water in wok over medium heat. Coat a 6-cup ring mold with oil. Sprinkle with sugar and rotate to distribute sugar evenly on bottom and sides of mold. Separate eggs. Sift flour with baking powder. In a large mixing bowl, beat egg whites until stiff. Add sugar a little at a time. Continue to beat until sugar is dissolved. In a separate bowl, beat egg yolks until light and lemon-colored. Fold into egg whites and sugar. Fold in flour mixture. Add extract. Pour into prepared mold. Place on rack in wok over simmering water. Cover loosely with a sheet of foil. Cover wok. Steam for 40 to 45 minutes, or until a knife inserted in center comes out clean. Cake will shrink slightly from mold. Remove from wok and let stand a few seconds. Place a cake rack over mold and holding rack and mold together invert to unmold. Dust lightly with powdered sugar. Cool to room temperature before slicing. Makes 6 to 8 servings.

Orange-Lemon Pudding

A truly heavenly dessert.

Butter for ring mold
Sugar for ring mold
1/2 cup chopped candied lemon peel
1/4 cup orange liqueur or orange juice
1/4 cup butter, softened
1/2 cup sugar
2 eggs
1 cup flour
2 teaspoons baking powder
1/4 cup fine dry bread crumbs
1/4 cup orange juice
Mandarin-Orange Sauce, see below

Mandarin-Orange Sauce:

1/2 cup sugar
2 tablespoons cornstarch
1 (11-oz.) can mandarin oranges
1/2 cup orange juice

Generously butter a 6-cup ring mold and sprinkle with sugar. Rotate mold to distribute sugar evenly on sides and bottom. Combine candied lemon peel and 1/4 cup orange liqueur or orange juice. Set aside. In a large bowl, cream butter and sugar until light and fluffy. Add eggs and beat well to blend. Sift flour and baking powder together; combine with bread crumbs. Alternately add flour mixture and 1/4 cup orange juice to batter. Fold in lemon-peel mixture. Pour into prepared mold. Place on rack in wok over simmering water. Cover wok and steam for 45 minutes. Invert to unmold and serve warm or cold with Mandarin-Orange Sauce. Makes 6 servings.

Mandarin-Orange Sauce:

In a large saucepan, combine sugar and cornstarch. Add juice from mandarin oranges and orange juice. Stir until smooth. Heat to boiling, stirring constantly, until thickened. Add mandarin orange sections. Serve warm over pudding.

Steam-Baked Apples

Makes beautifully glazed apples.

4 tablespoons prepared mincemeat
2 tablespoons orange juice
4 medium tart apples
1 cup boiling water
1/4 cup sugar
Peel from 1/2 lemon
Sour cream or whipped cream, for garnish

Mix mincemeat with orange juice. Peel top third of apples, reserve peelings. Core apples and fill with mincemeat. Place peelings, boiling water, sugar and lemon peel in baking dish. Stir to dissolve sugar. Add apples. Place on rack in wok over simmering water. Cover and steam for 30 minutes or until apples are tender. Baste occasionally while steaming. Cool in cooking liquid, basting frequently. Serve warm or cold with sour cream or whipped cream. Makes 4 servings.

Rum Cake

Rich, moist and fabulous!

Butter for loaf pan
Sugar for loaf pan
1 cup butter, room temperature
1-2/3 cup sugar
5 eggs
2 cups cake flour, sifted
2 teaspoons baking powder
1/4 cup rum or rum extract
1 cup boiling water, if necessary
1 cup Rum Glaze, see below
Whipped cream, if desired

Rum Glaze:

1/2 cup brown sugar, firmly packed
2 tablespoons water
1/2 cup light rum

Butter a 9-1/2" x 5-1/2" x 2" loaf pan. Sprinkle with sugar and tilt pan to distribute sugar evenly. Cream butter and sugar in a large mixing bowl until light and fluffy. Add eggs one at a time, beating well after each addition. Sift flour with baking powder. Add flour mixture to batter alternately with rum or rum extract, beating well after each addition. Pour into prepared pan and place on rack in wok over simmering water. Cover wok and steam 1 hour and 30 minutes. Uncover wok after 1 hour of cooking and, if necessary, add 1 cup boiling water. Remove cake from wok. Pour Rum Glaze over cake while still in pan. Cool and remove to a serving platter. Garnish with whipped cream if desired. Makes 8 to 10 servings.

Rum Glaze:

Combine brown sugar with water in a small pan. Cook over medium heat until sugar has melted. Stir in rum and pour over cake as directed.

Pineapple Flan

A delicate custard with a caramelized sauce.

4 tablespoons sugar
4 slices canned pineapple
2 maraschino cherries, cut in half
4 eggs
1/2 cup milk
1/2 cup sugar
1/2 teaspoon vanilla

In a small saucepan, melt sugar until it becomes a golden syrup. Pour equal amounts of syrup into 4 half-cup custard cups. Tilt each cup, coating sides evenly with syrup until syrup is almost hard. Place a slice of pineapple in bottom of each cup. Put a half cherry, cut-side up, in the center of each pineapple slice. Beat eggs with milk, sugar and vanilla until well blended. Fill each cup with mixture. Place in a shallow dish on rack in wok over simmering water. Cover loosely with foil. Cover wok and steam about 30 minutes until custard is firm. Remove from wok and turn custards out onto serving plates. Serve warm or cold. Makes 4 servings.

Coat the inside of a custard cup with melted sugar. After the sugar coating hardens, place a slice of pineapple in the bottom of the custard cup. Place a cherry half in the center of the pineapple slice.

Fill each custard cup with the egg mixture. Place in a shallow dish on the rack in the wok over simmering water. Cover loosely and steam.

Imperial Ice-Cream Cake

A special dessert for a special day.

Butter for loaf pan
Sugar for loaf pan
5 eggs, separated
1 cup sugar
2 tablespoons kirsch liqueur or 1 teaspoon almond
   or vanilla extract
1 cup sifted cake flour
1 teaspoon baking powder
1 pint strawberry ice cream
1 pint pistachio ice cream
1/2 pint heavy cream
1 pint heavy cream
1/4 cup sugar
1 oz. semi-sweet chocolate
Maraschino cherries, cut in half, for garnish

Generously butter a 9-1/2" x 5-1/2" loaf pan. Sprinkle with
sugar. Fill wok with water to just under rack. Place over
heat while preparing batter for cake. Beat egg whites until
stiff. Fold in 1 cup of sugar. Beat yolks with kirsch liqueur
or almond or vanilla extract until light and lemon-colored.
Add to beaten egg whites. Combine flour and baking
powder. Fold into beaten-egg mixture. Spoon into
prepared pan. Place on rack in wok over simmering water.
Cover and steam for 30 to 35 minutes or until firm.
Remove from wok, cool slightly. Place a cake rack over
pan and, holding pan and rack firmly together, invert and
remove pan. Cool cake completely. Using a serrated knife,
cut cake horizontally into 3 thin layers. Wrap each layer
and refrigerate until ready to use. Place each pint of ice
cream in a separate bowl and soften slightly. Whip 1/2 pint

of heavy cream until stiff. Fold half of whipped cream into each flavor of ice cream. Line bottom and sides of 2 loaf pans with foil. Bring foil up and over sides of pans. Spoon one flavor of each ice-cream mixture into bottom of each pan. Cover and place in freezer until very firm.

To assemble cake:

Place 1 layer of cake on a small foil-covered breadboard or baking sheet. Using foil on each side of pan, lift frozen strawberry ice cream out of pan and invert it over cake layer. Cover with second cake layer. Place pistachio layer on top. Cover with third cake layer. Place assembled cake in freezer while you beat 1 pint heavy cream until stiff. Fold in 1/4 cup sugar. Frost cake with sweetened whipped cream, covering it completely. With a small sharp knife scrape thin slivers of chocolate onto top of cake. Use maraschino-cherry halves for a border around bottom and sides of cake. Return cake to freezer until frozen solid. Wrap in foil and store in freezer. Remove from freezer 15 minutes before serving. Slice with a sharp serrated knife. Makes 8 to 10 servings.

Mocha-Nut Pudding

For chocolate lovers, a special coffee-flavored chocolate pudding.

Butter for ring mold
Sugar for ring mold
3 tablespoons butter, softened
3/4 cup sugar
2 eggs, separated
3/4 cup flour
2 teaspoons baking powder
1/4 cup cocoa
2 tablespoons fine dry bread crumbs
1/3 cup milk
2 tablespoons coffee
1/2 cup finely chopped walnuts
Orange Liqueur Sauce, see below

Orange-Liqueur Sauce:

1/2 cup sugar
2 eggs
2 tablespoons orange liqueur
1/2 cup heavy cream
1 teaspoon grated orange peel

Generously butter a 6-cup ring mold and sprinkle with sugar. Rotate to distribute sugar evenly over bottom and sides of mold. In a large mixing bowl, cream butter with sugar until light and fluffy. Add egg yolks and blend well. Sift flour with baking powder and cocoa; combine with bread crumbs. Mix milk with coffee. Alternately add flour mixture and milk mixture to batter. Blend well after each addition. Stir in walnuts. Beat egg whites until stiff; fold into batter. Pour into prepared mold. Place on rack in wok over simmering water. Cover wok and steam for 45 minutes. Invert to unmold. Serve warm or cold with Orange-Liqueur Sauce. Makes 6 servings.

Orange-Liqueur Sauce:

Combine sugar and eggs in top of double boiler over barely simmering water. Stir until sugar dissolves. Beat with a rotary beater until mixture thickens and triples in volume. Remove from heat; stir in liqueur. Beat until cooled to room temperature. Whip cream until very stiff, fold into sauce. Fold in orange peel. Chill until ready to serve.

Marmalade Pudding Cake

Try this delicious dessert with sweetened whipped cream.

Butter for ring mold
Sugar for ring mold
1 cup orange marmalade
1/4 cup butter, room temperature
2/3 cup sugar
2 eggs, well beaten
1 cup cake flour, sifted
1-1/2 teaspoons baking powder
1/4 cup milk
1/4 cup hot water

Lightly butter a 6-cup ring mold and sprinkle with sugar. Rotate to distribute evenly. Spoon marmalade over bottom of mold. In a mixing bowl, cream butter with sugar. Add eggs and beat well to blend. Sift flour with baking powder. Add alternately to batter with milk and hot water. Blend well and pour into prepared mold. Place on rack in wok over simmering water. Cover wok and steam for 35 to 40 minutes or until a knife inserted in the center comes out clean. Invert at once onto serving plate to unmold. Serve warm or cold. Makes 6 servings.

Old-Fashioned Deep-Fried Apple Pies

Made fast and easy in your old-fangled, new-fangled wok.

3 cups peeled and sliced tart apples
1/4 cup water
1/4 cup apple cider
1/3 cup sugar
1/2 teaspoon cinnamon
1/8 teaspoon nutmeg
6 frozen patty shells, thawed but still cold
Butter slivers
Oil for deep-frying
Powdered sugar

In a large saucepan, combine apples, water and cider. Cover and cook over low heat for 15 minutes or until tender. Cool to room temperature. Remove apple slices and drain. Place in a bowl. Mix together sugar, cinnamon and nutmeg. On a floured board, roll out patty shells to

1/8-inch thickness. Cut out rounds using a 3- to 3-1/2-inch cutter. Each rolled-out patty shell will yield 2 pastry rounds. Discard leftovers. Place about 2 tablespoons apple mixture on each pastry round. Dot with butter slivers. Moisten half the edge of each round with water. Fold the other half of round over filling. To seal, press edges together with fork tines. Pour oil in wok to a 3-inch center depth. Heat to 375°F (191°C). Fry pies in hot oil until golden brown, about 3 minutes. With tongs turn pies several times during cooking. Do not pierce. Drain over wok for a few seconds before placing on paper towels. Sprinkle with powdered sugar. Serve warm. Makes 12 individual pies.

Rice Croquettes With Apricot Sauce

Sweet and crisp.

1 cup long-grain rice, not instant or precooked
Water
2-1/2 cups milk
6 tablespoons sugar
1 teaspoon vanilla
3 egg yolks, slightly beaten
1 egg
1 tablespoon oil
1-1/2 cups fine dry cookie crumbs
Oil for frying
Apricot Sauce, see below

Apricot Sauce:

1 (1-lb.) can apricot halves with syrup
3 tablespoons powdered sugar
1/2 cup kirsch liqueur

Wash rice under cold water. Place in large pan and cover with water. Bring to a boil and cook for 5 minutes. Drain in a colander and rinse with cold water. Set aside. Pour milk in a large pan and heat to boiling. Add rice, lower heat and cover pan. Steam for 45 minutes to 1 hour or until tender and all liquid has evaporated. Remove from heat. Stir in sugar, vanilla and egg yolks. Cool slightly. Spoon the rice into a shallow pan. Chill until firm. Form into croquettes or balls. Slightly beat 1 egg with oil. Roll croquettes or balls in cookie crumbs; dip into beaten egg and roll in crumbs again. Chill well. Heat oil in wok to 375°F (191°C). Fry chilled croquettes a few at a time until golden brown. Drain on paper towels. Serve warm or at room temperature with Apricot Sauce. Makes 16 to 18 croquettes.

Apricot Sauce:

Combine apricots, powdered sugar and kirsch liqueur in an electric blender. Blend at high speed to puree.

Winter-Fruit Compote au Kirsch

A dessert that really glamorizes dried fruit.

2 cups mixed dried fruit
    apples, pears, peaches and plums
1 cup kirsch liqueur
1 cup sugar
1/2 cup slivered almonds

Place fruit in a shallow non-metal baking dish. Pour kirsch over fruit, sprinkle evenly with sugar. Allow to marinate for 2 to 3 hours. Place on rack in wok over simmering water. Cover wok and steam for 1 hour or until fruit is very tender. Sprinkle with almonds. Serve warm or chilled. Makes 6 servings.

Rum-Raisin Pudding

Lusciously rich.

Butter for ring mold
Sugar for ring mold
1/4 cup butter, softened
1/2 cup brown sugar, firmly packed
1 egg
1 cup flour
1 teaspoon baking powder
1/2 cup fine dry bread crumbs
1/4 cup milk
1/4 cup rum

1/2 cup molasses
1/2 cup chopped pecans
1/3 cup raisins
Hard Sauce, see below

Hard Sauce:

3 tablespoons butter
3/4 cup sifted powdered sugar
4 tablespoons rum

Generously butter a 6-cup ring mold and sprinkle with sugar. Rotate to distribute sugar evenly over the bottom and sides of mold. In a large mixing bowl, cream butter with sugar until light and smooth. Add egg and beat to blend. Sift flour with baking powder, combine with bread crumbs. Mix milk, rum and molasses together. Alternately add flour mixture and milk mixture to batter. Blend well after each addition. Fold in pecans and raisins. Pour into prepared mold. Place on rack in wok over simmering water. Cover wok. Steam for 45 minutes. Invert to unmold and serve warm or at room temperature with Hard Sauce. Makes 6 servings.

Hard Sauce:

In a small saucepan, melt butter. Remove from heat and stir in powdered sugar and rum. Chill until firm. If desired, pat out on pastry board and cut into star shapes. Chill until ready to serve.

Brandied Apple Pudding

A rich holiday dessert.

Butter for ring mold.
Sugar for ring mold
1/4 cup butter, room temperature
1/2 cup brown sugar, firmly packed
1 egg
1 cup all-purpose flour, sifted
1 teaspoon baking powder
1/4 teaspoon baking soda
1/2 cup fine dry bread crumbs
1/4 cup milk
1/4 cup brandy or cider
1/4 cup molasses
1 medium tart apple, peeled, cored and coarsely chopped
1/2 cup raisins
Brandy Sauce, see below

Brandy Sauce:

2 egg yolks
1/3 cup sugar
1/4 cup brandy or brandy extract
1/2 cup heavy cream

Generously butter a 6-cup ring mold. Sprinkle with sugar, rotating to distribute sugar evenly over bottom and sides of mold. In a large mixing bowl, cream butter with sugar, add egg and beat to blend. Sift flour with baking powder and baking soda. Combine with bread crumbs. Mix milk, brandy or cider and molasses together. Alternately add flour mixture and milk mixture to batter. Blend after each addition. Stir in chopped apples and raisins. Pour into prepared mold and place on rack in wok over simmering water. Cover wok and steam for 45 minutes. Invert to unmold. Serve warm or at room temperature topped with Brandy Sauce. Makes 6 servings.

Brandy Sauce:

Place egg yolks and sugar in top half of double boiler over simmering water. Beat with a rotary beater until about triple in volume. Remove from heat. Add brandy or brandy extract and beat to blend. Cover surface of sauce with wax paper to keep film from forming. Refrigerate until chilled. Beat cream until stiff and fold into chilled sauce. Refrigerate until ready to use.

Pears Cardinal

Sweet raspberry sauce over blushing pears.

6 firm ripe pears
Red food coloring
2 (10-oz.) pkg. frozen raspberries, thawed
2 tablespoons sugar
2 teaspoons cornstarch dissolved in 2 tablespoons water
1/4 cup kirsch liqueur

Place pears upright on rack in wok over simmering water.
Cover wok. Steam about 10 to 15 minutes, depending on
the ripeness of the pears. Remove pears from wok. Hold
each under cold running water and gently rub off skin. Rub
one side of each pear with a little red food coloring, to give
it a blush. Refrigerate, covered, until well chilled. Puree
raspberries in a blender. If desired, strain out seeds. In a
saucepan, bring puree to a boil. Stir in sugar and dissolved
cornstarch. Stir until mixture thickens. Remove from heat
and add kirsch liqueur. Refrigerate until well chilled. Place
pears in individual serving bowls. Spoon sauce over and
around each. Makes 6 servings.

Mocha Velvet Cake

For a fabulous dessert, split this cake into 3 layers and spread each layer with peppermint ice cream. Smooth whipped cream over the top and sprinkle with crushed peppermint candy. Mmmmm.

Oil for loaf pan
Sugar for loaf pan
1 cup butter, softened
1-2/3 cups sugar
5 eggs
2 cups sifted cake flour
2 teaspoons baking powder
1 tablespoon cocoa
1 tablespoon instant coffee
2 tablespoons very hot water
2 tablespoons brandy extract

Oil a 9-1/2" x 5-1/2" x 2-1/2" loaf pan. Sprinkle with sugar; tilt pan to coat sides and bottom evenly with sugar. In a large mixing bowl, cream butter with sugar until light and fluffy. Add eggs one at a time, beating well after each addition. Sift flour, baking powder and cocoa together. Dissolve instant coffee in 2 tablespoons hot water; combine with brandy extract. Alternately add flour and dissolved coffee to batter, beating thoroughly after each addition. Fill wok with water to just below rack; bring to a simmer. Pour batter into prepared pan. Place on rack in wok over simmering water. Cover wok and steam for 1 hour. Uncover; add additional hot water as needed. Cover and steam for 30 minutes. Invert on a cake rack and remove pan. Cool before slicing. Makes 8 to 10 servings.

Mocha Sponge Cake

Coffee and chocolate blend for a fabulous flavor!

Butter for loaf pan
Sugar for loaf pan
5 eggs, room temperature
1 tablespoon instant coffee
2 tablespoons boiling water
1 cup flour
3 tablespoons cocoa
1 teaspoon baking powder
1 cup sugar
Powdered sugar, for garnish

Fill wok with water to just below rack; place over medium heat. Butter a 9-1/2" x 5-1/2" x 2-1/2" loaf pan and sprinkle with sugar. Tilt pan to distribute sugar evenly on sides and bottom. Separate eggs. Dissolve instant coffee in boiling water. Cool to room temperature. Sift flour with cocoa and baking powder and set aside. In a large bowl, beat egg whites until stiff. Add sugar, about 1/4 cup at a time, beating thoroughly after each addition. Beat yolks in a separate bowl until light and lemon-colored. Add dissolved instant coffee. Stir to blend. Fold into beaten egg whites. Fold in flour-cocoa mixture, about 1/4 cup at a time, blending lightly but thoroughly. Spoon batter into prepared pan. Place on rack in wok over simmering water. Cover wok and steam cake for 35 minutes, or until a knife inserted in center comes out clean. Remove from wok and let stand at room temperature about 2 minutes. Place cake rack over pan and, holding pan and rack firmly together, invert and remove pan. Cool cake before slicing. Dust with powdered sugar. Makes 6 to 8 servings.

Beignets a la New Orleans

Years ago women walked through the streets of New Orleans' ancient French quarter selling these spicy fried pastries from baskets balanced on their heads.

1 envelope dry yeast
3 tablespoons warm water
1/4 cup warm milk
4 cups cake flour
2 tablespoons sugar
1/2 teaspoon salt
1 teaspoon cinnamon
1-1/4 cups milk
3 eggs
3/4 cup butter, melted and cooled to room temperature
Oil for deep-frying
Powdered sugar

Butter a large bowl to hold the rising dough. In a medium-size bowl, dissolve yeast in warm water. Add 1/4 cup warm milk and 1 cup cake flour. Blend well. Cover bowl and let dough rise in a warm place about 30 minutes, or until double in bulk. In a large bowl sift the remaining 3 cups cake flour, sugar, salt and cinnamon. Add 1-1/4 cups milk, eggs and butter. Beat until thoroughly blended. Add dough mixture and mix to a soft dough. Transfer mixture into the buttered bowl. Cover and set aside in a warm place until double in bulk. Pour oil in wok to a center depth of about 3 inches. Heat to 375°F (191°C). Drop dough by teaspoons, a few at a time, into the hot oil. Fry about 2 minutes until deep golden brown. Drain on paper towels. Roll in powdered sugar. Serve warm. Makes about 36 beignets.

THREE GREAT JAPANESE DINNERS

This section gives you three great recipes that are representative of Japanese cuisine and have become favorites in many places around the world.

People who are already familiar with Japanese cooking in restaurants but have not prepared it at home will enjoy the recipes given here. For those who have never tried these foods, this section serves a double purpose. Please consider it an invitation to become acquainted with Japanese tastes and food-preparation methods. The recipes, instructions and photos will also serve as a guide, assuring success even if you have never cooked this way before.

For entertaining with an intimate and friendly atmosphere, these dishes are ideal. Food is cooked at the table, which generates a sense of well-being and mutual sharing even among strangers. For some of these dishes, guests participate in the cooking which contributes even more to the pleasant atmosphere of the occasion.

No one is completely at ease when preparing or eating foods with unpronounceable names. These names are not difficult, but for those who are unfamiliar with them, the following descriptions include a pronunciation guide.

Sukiyaki

Usually pronounced *sookey-aki*, this is basically a stir-fried dish with strips of meat. It's cooked at the table and served directly from the wok. One ingredient unfamiliar to Westerners is *tofu*, a high-protein bean curd that is a staple in the Japanese diet. It may be an acquired taste, like olives and caviar. Try it with an open mind.

Tempura

Pronounced *tem-poora*, this is the Japanese art of deep-frying which retains so little fat that the results are amazingly low in calories. Tempura foods are delicately crisp with a thin—almost transparent—batter coating. There is no greasy taste, just superb flavor.

Yase Nobe

Usually pronounced *yosa-nobby*. *Yase* translates roughly as a put-together variety of foods. *Nobe* is the Japanese word for foods cooked at the table in a simmering broth. Everyone cooks his or her own selection and the results are a good time and a great meal.

Sukiyaki

Naturally you want to make Japanese Sukiyaki in your wok. The high, even heat cooks beef and vegetables to perfection in minutes and the sloping sides make it easy to stir-fry the ingredients without spattering.

Sukiyaki is fun to make at the table—especially for a party. Arrange the ingredients on a long decorative platter or tray. Have a small pitcher of cooking oil at the table. Serve individual bowls of cooked rice and dipping sauce to each guest. Your wok, either electric or a conventional one placed over a portable burner, completes the table-top kitchen.

3 tablespoons oil
1 teaspoon sesame oil, if available
1-1/2 lbs. lean tender beef, sirloin or tenderloin, trimmed, sliced about 1/4-in. thick, cut in bite-size pieces
3 teaspoons sugar
3/4 cup thinly sliced green onions, white part only
1 small sweet potato, peeled, sliced thin, cut into "matchsticks"
1 white turnip, peeled, sliced thin, cut in pie-shaped wedges
1/2 lb. mushrooms, trimmed, cut lengthwise through stems into thin slices
6 tablespoons chicken broth
1/2 lb. Chinese cabbage or spinach leaves, trimmed and shredded
3 tablespoons soy sauce
3 cups hot cooked rice
1/2 lb. tofu or bean curd, cut into bite-size pieces
Dipping Sauce, see below

Dipping Sauce:

1/2 cup soy sauce
1/2 cup fresh lime juice
1/2 cup semi-sweet sherry

Heat 1 tablespoon of oil and a few drops of sesame oil in the wok over high heat. Add 1/3 of the meat and sprinkle with 1 teaspoon of the sugar. Stir-fry until meat is no longer pink. Add 1/3 each of the green onions, potatoes, turnips and mushrooms. Pour 2 tablespoons chicken broth over ingredients. Cover and steam for about 1 minute. Uncover and stir-fry about 30 seconds. Add 1/3 of the cabbage or spinach leaves. Cover and steam about 30 seconds; uncover and add 1 tablespoon soy sauce. Add 1/3 of tofu or bean-curd pieces. Stir-fry only until cabbage is crisp-tender. Serve a small portion to each guest. Cook another 1/3 of the ingredients after the first is eaten, and repeat with remaining ingredients. Makes 6 servings.

Dipping Sauce:

Combine ingredients and blend well.

How to Make Sukiyaki

Arrange the meat and vegetables to be cooked on a large platter.

Stir-fry 1/3 of the meat until it is no longer pink. Add sugar and green onions. Then add potatoes, turnips and mushrooms.

After steaming and stir-frying with other ingredients, serve small portions to your guests. Repeat the same cooking steps with another 1/3 of the ingredients.

Tempura

The secret of tempura cookery is to have the batter and the foods to be cooked icy cold and the cooking oil very hot, 375°F (191°C), measured with a deep-fat thermometer. If you don't have a deep-fat thermometer, test the temperature of the oil with a cube of bread. Toss the bread into the hot oil. If it sinks to the bottom, then immediately rises to the surface and turns golden brown in about 60 seconds—the oil is at the right heat.

Any number of foods can be used for tempura. Shrimp are superb but so are scallops. Less-expensive, firm, white fish fillets cut into bite-size pieces also work well. Vegetables are delicious fried this way. Some of the best are broccoli flowerets, carrot and zucchini sticks, small whole mushrooms and sliced sweet potato. The only vegetables to avoid in tempura frying are watery ones, such as tomatoes, cabbage and cucumber. For a surprise taste try tempura-fried chunks of fresh pineapple or crisp apple slices.

A tempura party is fun for everyone, including the hostess and host. Bring your wok to the table and place it over a portable burner especially designed to hold it. Or, use an electric wok. Have the cooking oil handy in a small pitcher. Ice water, plus all ingredients for preparing the batter should be on a small tray and the platter of cold ready-to-cook foods must be nearby.

Pour oil to a 3-inch center depth—about 3 cups of oil in a 14-inch wok. Start heating it *before* you prepare the batter.

The real key to a perfect batter is to make it just before using so it stays ice-cold. Don't try to cook too many pieces of food at one time. Overloading chills the oil and causes a soggy crust. Cook one small serving at a time: one or two shrimp, a scallop, a piece of fish and a few assorted vegetables.

Don't wait until all foods are prepared to serve everyone. Tempura party etiquette calls for serving guests *as the food is prepared*. It's quick cooking, so no one will have to wait long. Give each guest a bowl of dipping sauce and, if desired, a small bowl of rice. Chopsticks are fun but not everyone can manage them, so have forks handy, especially if you are serving rice. Actually, tempura foods need no implements—fingers are the best tools. Ice-cold beer or iced tea are perfect accompaniments.

This recipe is one I use often. You can add to or subtract from the list of seafood and vegetables to suit your own taste and that of your guests.

1 lb. jumbo shrimp, cleaned, deveined
1/2 lb. scallops
1/2 lb. fish fillets, cut crosswise in 1/2-in. strips
1 large zucchini, trimmed and cut in 1/2-in. slices
2 small carrots, peeled, cut lengthwise in 1/2-in.-thick
   sticks
12 medium mushrooms, trimmed
1 large sweet potato, peeled, sliced in 1/2-in.-thick
   rounds, rounds quartered
1 small bunch broccoli, trimmed, broken into
   flowerets
1/2 cup flour, sifted
1 tablespoon cornstarch
1 teaspoon baking powder
1 egg white
Ice water
3 cups peanut oil for frying
Dipping Sauce, see below

Dipping Sauce:

1/2 cup soy sauce
1/4 cup sweet sauterne
1 cup chicken broth

Arrange all seafood, fish and vegetables in an attractive design on one or more platters. Refrigerate until ready to cook. When ready to prepare tempura, assemble all foods and necessary ingredients near wok. Heat oil in wok while preparing batter. Combine flour, cornstarch and baking powder in a mixing bowl. Blend well. Add egg white and enough ice water to make a batter about the consistency of heavy cream. Stir, *do not beat*, to blend. Don't worry if there are a few lumps as they will disappear as you use the batter. When oil is heated to 375°F (191°C), start frying the chilled foods. Dip a piece of fish, shellfish or vegetable into the batter; drain briefly over the bowl then lower into hot oil. Fry until lightly browned. Place on a paper towel to drain. Fry only a few pieces at a time so oil temperature remains consistently hot. Fry an assortment to make one serving: a few pieces of seafood plus a variety of vegetables. Serve immediately. Makes 6 to 8 servings.

Dipping Sauce:

Combine all ingredients. Mix well and pour into individual bowls.

How to Make Tempura

Arrange the vegetables and seafood on a large platter. Refrigerate until ready to cook so the food will be icy cold.

Bring all the ingredients to the table. While you prepare the batter, the oil can be heating in the wok. Combine batter ingredients and stir to blend. Do not beat.

Dip the chilled foods in the cold batter and fry in very hot oil, 375°F (191°C). Cook only a few pieces of food at a time so the chilled foods won't lower the temperature of the oil.

Yase Nobe

This menu is just one example of a *nobe* dish. You can add items for more variety or subtract for a less-elaborate meal. While almost all meats, shellfish and vegetables can be used, some are more suitable for *nobe*-style cooking. All food is cut into bite-size pieces or thinly sliced. You can use beef, veal or pork. Seafoods could be oysters or clams.

For raw vegetables, green or white onions are almost always included. Good, too, are tender young spinach leaves, watercress and carrots. Pumpkin (parboiled in advance for 5 minutes) or broccoli flowerets (parboiled in advance for 2 minutes) are also flavorful additions.

Some exotic, but not essential additions can be found at a Japanese grocery store or in the Oriental section of your supermarket. Try Japanese dried mushrooms. Soak them in cold water for 10 to 15 minutes before using. Bean-thread noodles (pour boiling water over them and let stand 15 minutes before draining) and already-broiled or fried-canned bean curd, along with the more easily obtainable snow peas and bamboo shoots, are interesting variations.

The broth recipe is not authentically Japanese, but it's equally flavorful.

Each person uses chopsticks or a skewer such as used for fondue to place pieces of food into the pot and recover them when cooked as desired. Then a quick dip into the dipping sauce, a moment to cool so you don't burn your tongue, and the taste is delightful.

4 cups fat-free chicken broth
1-1/2 cups water
1/2 cup sweet sauterne
2 chicken breasts, skinned, boned and cut in bite-size
    pieces
1 lb. shrimp, cleaned, deveined

1/2 lb. firm white fish fillets, cod or bass
8 to 12 green onions, trimmed
2 small white turnips, peeled, sliced and parboiled
   5 minutes
1 medium-size sweet potato, peeled and sliced thin
Sprigs of watercress
1/2 lb. tofu or bean curd, cut in bite-size pieces
3 cups hot cooked rice
Dipping Sauce, see below

Dipping Sauce:

1 cup light soy sauce
1/2 cup dry sherry

Combine broth, water and sauterne and bring to a simmer at the table in an electric wok or a conventional wok over a portable burner. Arrange all foods except rice and Dipping Sauce in attractive designs on 2 or more platters. Place cooked rice in individual serving bowls. Give each guest a small bowl of Dipping Sauce. The meal is ready to begin. The guests choose their own food from the platters and drop it into the simmering broth for a few minutes. When cooked, the food is dipped in sauce and eaten with rice. When all food has been cooked, the broth is served and can be enjoyed with a bit of rice and Dipping Sauce to enhance the rich flavor. Makes 6 servings.

Dipping Sauce:

Combine soy sauce and sherry and mix well. Pour into individual bowls.

How to Make Yase Nobe

Arrange the ingredients to be cooked on a large platter. All foods should be cut in bite-sized pieces or sliced thinly.

Carefully lower the pieces of food into the hot broth and let them simmer for a few minutes.

Remove the foods from the broth and dip into Dipping Sauce. Rice is the perfect accompaniment.

CONVERSION TO METRIC MEASURE

When you know	Symbol	Multiply by	To find	Symbol
teaspoons	tsp	5	milliliters	ml
tablespoons	tbsp	15	milliliters	ml
fluid ounces	fl oz	30	milliliters	ml
cups	c	0.24	liters	l
pints	pt	0.47	liters	l
quarts	qt	0.95	liters	l
ounces	oz	28	grams	g
pounds	lb	0.45	kilograms	kg
Fahrenheit	°F	5/9 (after subtracting 32)	Celsius	C
inches	in	2.54	centimeters	cm
feet	ft	30.5	centimeters	cm

Sincere thanks to Mrs. Gafford Pearce, who helped test many of the recipes in this book.

LIQUID MEASURE TO MILLILITERS

1/4 teaspoon	=	1.25 milliliters
1/2 teaspoon	=	2.5 milliliters
3/4 teaspoon	=	3.75 milliliters
1 teaspoon	=	5 milliliters
1¼ teaspoons	=	6.25 millileters
1½ teaspoons	=	7.5 milliliters
1¾ teaspoons	=	8.75 milliliters
2 teaspoons	=	10 milliliters
1 tablespoon	=	15 milliliters
2 tablespoons	=	30 milliliters

FAHRENHEIT TO CELSIUS

F	C
200°	93°
225°	107°
250°	121°
275°	135°
300°	149°
325°	163°
350°	177°
375°	191°
400°	204°
425°	218°
450°	232°
475°	246°
500°	260°

LIQUID MEASURE TO LITERS

1/4 cup	=	0.06 liters
1/2 cup	=	0.12 liters
3/4 cup	=	0.18 liters
1 cup	=	0.24 liters
1¼ cups	=	0.3 liters
1½ cups	=	0.36 liters
2 cups	=	0.48 liters
2½ cups	=	0.6 liters
3 cups	=	0.72 liters
3½ cups	=	0.84 liters
4 cups	=	0.96 liters
4½ cups	=	1.08 liters
5 cups	=	1.2 liters
5½ cups	=	1.32 liters

INDEX

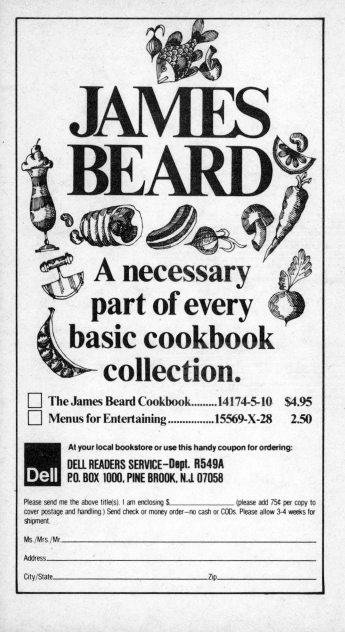

What you eat can make and keep you well.

LENDON SMITH, M.D.

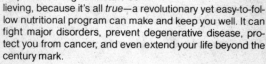

You are what you eat. How often have you heard this cliche…and wondered? Well stop wondering and start believing, because it's all *true*—a revolutionary yet easy-to-follow nutritional program can make and keep you well. It can fight major disorders, prevent degenerative disease, protect you from cancer, and even extend your life beyond the century mark.

An important section, arranged alphabetically, describes various signs, symptoms, and conditions and explains how you can use nutrition to cure them.

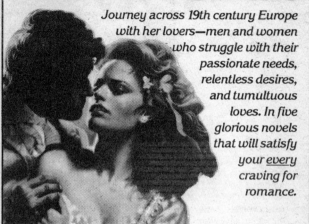